A Touchy Subject

Beth James

Editing, design, typesetting and publishing by UK Book Publishing
www.ukbookpublishing.com
ISBN: 978-1-914195-42-6

For my parents
Betty and Edwin

Making a Meal of It

15.01.17

Dear Cassie,

Fried mince and onions is not chilli con carne, I admit, but that is the risk of employing a supply teacher in the food technology department with catering qualifications based solely on their ability to operate a Bunsen burner.

Alas, the school's newly appointed food technology technician, Mrs Prendergast, whom you have yet to encounter, uninitiated in the art of turning a blind eye, or listed on the gas safe register, is not party to the 'beggars can't be choosers' supply teacher selection procedure.

As the school's longest serving supply teacher, tasked with teaching every secondary school subject known to the examination board at a moment's notice, it came as a shock to be charged with not knowing my onions by a presumptuous newcomer. Not know my onions. That's rich. I could write out the Allium cepa family tree.

Nonetheless, sixteen years' prior experience as a stay-at-home mum, not thirty incarcerated in the classroom, has prepared Mrs Prendergast, with great aplomb, to critically rule the food room roost. The cut-glass voice gaining the upper hand, resonantly, with the perfect dictation. However, from the art perspective, one score year and four months spent behind paint splattered walls, surely you will agree with me, there can only be room for the one unassailable classroom presence to dictate the orders.

The Year 9 pupils (thirteen – such a tricky age) were given the challenge of making a chilli con carne, something of a dog's dinner, but then again, that is the parental right to choose.

At the end of the lesson, when the pupils had filed out (singularly, calmly, and quietly – I don't endorse the scrum), my nemesis was stood on an imaginary podium, puffed up to full height, triumphantly waving a pupil's discarded bulging carrier bag aloft. No need for a medal, the victorious look in her eyes signalling 'I've got you' ample reward.

Forensic investigation of the much-hailed bag unearthed a cache of chopped onions and chopped red peppers (all elements of food technology must be sliced and diced at home, by parental hand, well in advance of the appointed mixing hour – technologically brilliant in that all aspects of the food preparation process bypasses the child), along with two unopened tin cans, one housing chopped tomatoes, the other kidney beans with chilli sauce. Indeed, every component needed to make chilli con carne bar the carne.

Some free-thinking pupil, devoid of the spice gene, had had the audacity (or genius) to modify the recipe to fried mince and onions, well, minus the onions (no need for onions on the hands), cleverly circumventing all the usual problems associated with not knowing a teaspoon from a tablespoon for ladling out the spice.

However, it's a slippery slope, Cassie, when pupils start experimenting and deviating from the modus operandi, especially when it gives credence to others that I may lack classroom observational skills. If I hadn't been soothing distressed vegetarians, unwilling to share a room with any form of mince, vegetarian or otherwise (Quorn brings tears to the eyes as well as the onions), or having to open nineteen cans of kidney beans due to a collective lack of mastery with a can opener (should have been twenty but found one hidden in the rubbish bin, observational skills on fire –interrogation unmasking another fussy eater, also with leanings more toward the carnivore), I might have spied the carne con carne before it marched from the room, thereby pre-empting a purist looking askance.

The lessons with the other year groups, conducted under gimlet eye, didn't fare much better. The wet behind the ears, despite a good towelling, Year 7s (eleven still an age of compliance) managed to spoil the broth quite naturally with the help of the woeful recipe, not one too many chiefs.

Five different vegetables – carrot and potato compulsory, the other three discretionary – all forms of mince prohibited, had to be boiled in a vat of water under the guise of soup making. Well, take it from me, a sprig of coriander (the finishing touch for the more discerning taste bud) isn't going to do the trick when the air glade has run out, the pupils hot on its heels looking greener than peas. Although to the carnivores in the room, 'all is forgiven'.

To get the most out of the soup making experience, a spell

in hospital beforehand is to be recommended. I have had this on good authority. The day after the cauldron-stirring exercise, a young man came to see me to say how much his mum, who had just left hospital, had enjoyed his efforts. I believe the exact words used upon seeing his gourmet delight were, 'that's all I need'. It is gratifying to know that occasionally we provide a much-appreciated service. If only I had faith in the soup's recuperative powers I would bottle you some, but using a flask with a wider neck opening than a pencil because that entailed its own set of problems.

My husband, Stuart, is complaining that I smell 'funny' (fragrance of boiled cabbage) and Mrs Prendergast, seemingly traumatised one week after the event, is still lamenting the state of 'her' food technology room floor. The stress is getting me so hot under the collar – could possibly be the menopause, or multiple ovens or hobs in use simultaneously – that a couple of the pupils have started asking me if I need the services of 'Eloise of Lourdes', the school welfare officer. A psychiatrist in a darkened room wouldn't go amiss, but how I could relax or recline with a mop handle up the – let's say – indecorously placed is quite another matter.

The 'fruit fusion', an upmarket rebranding of fruit salad, (many areas identified and highlighted for improvement) was another Year 7 task requiring the bronze personal survival badge and a handy pair of pyjamas. The vegetables not the only ones to land in hot water. The fruits, a harmonious blend of colour contrasting soft and hard fruits, of the pupils' choosing, should have been floating in fruit juice provided by the small carton, not the family sized bumper pack for the pineapple chunk with scales. Transportation of the 'fruit fusion' home, for parental approval, an exercise suited only to those thinking of a tight-roping career.

Back on terra firma, I had hoped that relations between teacher and technician would take a turn for the better. What folly. The offensive word yet to be uttered. When I asked Mrs Prendergast if she could kindly get out the 'bun' trays, in preparation for the Year 7 'bun' making practical, you would have thought I'd grown two heads and was an anathema to the world of small cakes. 'Bun' is clearly not a word to be bandied about lightly, Cassie, its Yorkshire pronunciation – not altogether unexpected in the Yorkshire comprehensive school – an egregious affront to the more refined ear. So, with the vowels betraying me, it was understandably daunting to request the muffin trays for the 'healthy muffins' bake. However, even with elocution lessons, I doubt I would have been awarded top marks for making genteel 'cupcakes' any better.

The Year 8 contentious 'healthy muffin' making exercise is something of a mystery. The health benefits not immediately obvious when the services of the emergency dentist are required. The Mohs scale of hardness is usually reserved for the geography lesson, not the grading of rock buns masquerading as muffins.

To receive a clean bill of health, the healthy muffin must have its regular, tried and tested, ingredients substituted with less palatable choices, but lowering the fat content (semi skimmed for full fat), banning the sugar, and bumping up the fibre (porridge oats for flour) are recipes for disaster.

There's no sweetness and light for the muffin any more than there is with Mrs Prendergast.

As a child I was subjected to skimmed milk before it had graced the market, my brother racing downstairs every morning to skim off the unpasteurised (we lived dangerously) milk's creamy head, no consideration for the shake. My parents were oblivious, only concerned with the protein requirements of the 'ever growing lad', leaving his two sisters not growing, stunned and stunted. My mother was blinded by her middle child theories, some sorry notion of how difficult it is for a boy to be wedged between two girls. A notion that has forever left my brother the cat with the cream.

Pupils these days, through inculcation and indoctrination of the healthy eating message, shun clotted cream as if it could clog the arteries on the spot (is there anything more glorious with homemade jam and scone?) but giving the chocolate chip the cold shoulder is an entirely different kettle of fish. At the pupils' bidding, chocolate chips, not the high antioxidant, life-prolonging blueberries, as recommended by an ineffective teacher, remained the only unaltered original feature on the ingredients list.

Ergo, considering the lack of available teaching talent, Cassie, it must be a tremendous relief to know that the school has managed to drum up a specialist art supply teacher to teach your own classes, aged from eleven to sixteen, including GCSE, during your period of absence. The Real McCoy won't be reduced to demonstrating brush strokes and technique with a pastry brush and cake decorating palette knife, with yet another raised eyebrow from the corner. Although this time

I think the raised eyebrow more to do with not rising to the occasion than speaking 'Dutch' in Yorkshire. It's easily done, missing out half a teaspoon of baking powder in the year eight Dutch Apple Cake demonstration when concentrating on getting the mouth around Hollandse appeltaart, to avoid a further swipe at the crumbs.

The redoubtable Mrs Prendergast is fortunate that I didn't launch into Double Dutch (the pill and condom combined) having carried out safe sex more times than I care to remember. There is more than one string to the supply teacher's bow, although I wouldn't wish to divulge that I was good at plucking for fear of further misunderstanding.

I wish I could tell you all these things in person, as I have done for many years, sitting in your art room for a snatched chat at lunchtime. Now I will be reduced to writing, but take it as gospel that it will be the dated letter and not the modern indecipherable text. Nothing could reduce me to texting – I have far too much to get off my chest. From school issues to the home front, confidentiality permitting, I intend, my dear friend, to keep you in the loop. Matters of school discipline will be carefully avoided – far too depressing, we can't all rely on the giant sweetie jar. However, I will have my eye out, rest assured, for the unattached male, aged forty to fifty, from parent, to teacher, to Ofsted Inspector, strolling into school unawares. Anything to help alleviate your current single status; but so far there is nothing of interest to report. No doubt my own children, Alex and Meg, will feature in future correspondence, similarly single, 'not even looking', but now in their twenties it is time that they did.

I can't name names for obvious reasons but before I sign off I thought you would be delighted to know that one of your more empathetic Year 10 form members is desperately missing you and requests daily, nay demands, the date of your return. The young man in question cannot gain access to his locker with the regularity that he requires and needs you back urgently to rectify the situation. He's not the only one desperately missing you, frantically picking the lock. I can't find the key for the filing cabinet housing the chocolate Florentines stocks that we share, so either kindly make haste or post it back.

Yours truly

Beth

PS I could always give petits gateaux ou gateaux petits a shot to win approval. What do you think? If only the French could make their minds up whether they want it back or front.

Scenting Trouble

05.02.17

Dear Cassie,

Well, you will be relieved to hear that I have been replaced in the food technology department, hopefully by an expert with an eye for the accurate fluid measurement and an ability to control the pupils' breathing rate.

A new carbon dioxide monitoring machine has been placed in the food room to measure air quality. No prizes for guessing that it could only be on my watch that the device started to emit critical, last gasp readings, signalling 'throw open all windows immediately', lack of a window pole notwithstanding.

Other than organising and hosting a 'Hold the Breath' competition (don't tempt me) – first to a dead faint winning the prize – or barring the use of the gas cookers in the cooking process, it is difficult to know how to purify and remedy a situation that I find myself held accountable for.

A methane monitor, with a warning alarm for 'clear the room urgently', would be perfectly understandable. There should be one of those in every classroom scenting trouble, or even a detector for the more lethal carbon monoxide, but carbon dioxide doesn't register on the nasal scale. As a vital component of fire extinguishers, 'one would think' (Mrs Prendergast's influence is telling) that a pall of carbon dioxide in the air would come in quite handy for damping, not fanning, the cooking flames.

So, out of the frying pan and into the fiery furnace of Religious, Personal and Social Education, RPSE, and its side kick subject PSE.

I was too polite to say to Mrs Drinkwater, the school's operations manager – specialist area of expertise: dragging the nearest available daily rate supply teacher into school without bung, bribe, or beverage (do as I say, not as I do) – that I would like to work in that department as much as having 'a hole in the head'.

If I am not feeding pupils, I am catering to their sexual needs. If the PSE lessons, up close and personal without the religious element, followed my mother's contraceptive advice of 'keep your knickers on at all times', pupils wouldn't be overdosing on sexually transmitted infections, STIs. I'm only surprised that there aren't a few 'Chlamydias' in the classroom, the sort that scathingly say, 'I only answer to Clammy on the register, don't you know anything?' Considering a teacher's ability to call out the register, without hesitation, consternation or mispronunciation, should be taken more seriously by parents jockeying for the top position in the 'notice my child' at all costs, naming game.

As it turned out, not every lesson was about planning a day's trip to the GUM clinic, formerly given the acronym CLAP in the days when a bun was called a bun, and milk was valued for its creamy head, not its homogenised whey; one or two lessons had a religious content to them.

Evaluating miracles (evaluating is more omnipresent in RPSE than God and is a compulsive disorder that must be carried out tirelessly every single lesson, regardless of the topic under study) featured highly. I was praying fervently that the lesson would follow PE where time keeping is less than punctilious, to help shorten the lesson, or for the overenthusiastic fire alarm testing pupil so that I could escape to line up in a rain sodden yard, minus coat, and umbrella, yet still grateful. Alas, my prayers were not answered, providing evidence for which side of the miracle argument I am on.

Mathematical miracles have also been in short supply. A day's teaching in the maths department provided the usual hunt for technical equipment, nothing too high brow such as a compass or protractor, more the basics of a pen and a pencil.

To begin the day, the head of maths, Mr Fitzsimmons – another new appointment (new term new faces), whom I had not been previously introduced to – waltzed into the room, threw a piece of paper onto the teacher's desk and said, 'That's the work for the day'. Not so much as a 'Good morning', 'How are you?' or even, 'Who are you?' Could have got wind that I double up as 'Typhoid Mary', I suppose, or that I get more than my fair share of syphilis (lessons not symptoms), but more likely, it was the typical dismissive attitude towards the 'second rate supply teacher' wearing the invisibility cloak. Either that or he was deliberately cutting the conversation short to keep the carbon dioxide levels down as air quality is as ripe in maths as it is in food technology.

However, the pupils are not doing their bit for global warming, blowing enough hot air throughout the day to melt the polar ice caps. It's a good job that you are out of earshot, Cassie, or you could be forgiven for thinking that 'shit' is a more appropriate and acceptable word for 'crap' (that's the RPSE evaluations doing the rounds again), the pronunciation of Plato is the same as an elevated area of flat land in geography and saintly Teresa May has left politics to take up the habit, possibly with a lump of coke lodged up the nose. If only the pupils could see beyond snorting or imbibing when it comes to the studying of solid fuels.

Correcting so many misconceptions, I have barely had time to read the relentless electronic messages bombarding an overworked 'in box', messages that seemingly proliferate by chain reaction. I will ty to keep you abreast of the most pressing communications but, understandably, can only spread word from the classified pages – 'Items most Wanted' or 'The Lost and Found'. It should keep your hand in. Always good to feel useful.

The food technology department is urgently seeking pasta machines. I know there is panic over Brexit, but do we really have to start making our own pasta when the Italians have mastered the knack? The Italians may well be a very excitable nation, with no observance or understanding of the laws and conventions associated with the use of the pedestrian crossing, but surely, we could negotiate. I think that we need to get our own house in order and learn to correctly boil English cabbage, within the 1956 clean air act of course, and peel and dice the humble potato before we get ahead of ourselves. When a requested medium potato, for the soup making process, can range in size from the glacial erratic to the pea gravel pebble, it means that the maths department has more to answer for than a lack of rulers and manners.

Mr Honeyman, King of the School Props department, urgently requires six ping pong balls for cherries on the Queen's tarts ('Alice in Wonderland' Production). One person with six, or six colleagues with one, he is not fussy, but donations only as they will be ruined. How true, and if only I could get my hands on half a dozen they wouldn't see the light of day.

I'm optimistic that Mr Honeyman's request for plumage feathers, ranging from three to twelve inches in autumnal colours, will be met, not so much for the seasonal interest as the certainty that some child will be on first name terms with either a Giant Ostrich or a Bee Hummingbird. Yes, you can add naturalist to my bow – the Bee Hummingbird is no longer than a bee, hence its name.

One of the English teachers has taken up space in the 'found' column. For once, not the usual old hat of keys, glasses, lanyards, or memory sticks, but a stamp found in the possession of a pupil. Not the stick-on kind, with adhesive in such short supply, but a reward yourself with the good comment kind. There's even photographic evidence of the suspected stolen stamp, with potential teachers being asked to step forward with proof of ownership. Well, I'm no Sherlock, but surely it would be easier to give the stamp a go, and if it prints 'well done in geography' you have narrowed it down to three. If it stamps 'great evaluation' divine inspiration will lead the way and 'inhale only' is self explanatory. Thankfully, one has not been reported missing from the food technology department or I would be hauled over the coals for that, solid fuels permitting now they are no longer in vogue and so pollutant emitting.

In the 'lost' column, a pair of small yellow fibreglass step ladders, with blue holster top, has gone 'walk about'. Any information as to the step ladders' whereabouts must be passed on immediately to Mr Mackenzie. Big Mac, grandiosely self titled, and officially the school accountant but with leanings towards odd job man, with electric drill rather than calculator always to hand, will be ruing the loss on two fronts. I would suggest a peek into one or two pencil cases having recently observed a pencil case in the form of a green alligator, that looked, quite frankly, built to size, lugubriously strewn across a desk eyeballing me. My husband says that I need to watch out over my surveillance worries and I've assured him that I am. 'Don't Miss a Trick' Prendergast won't trip me up with the use of the gator cam.

The school welfare officer, 'Eloise of Lourdes', in her secondary capacity as 'Mistress of the Missing' (Big Mac is not the only one to multitask), has reported that twenty-two of the twenty-five especially reserved school mugs, for the full school governors, have gone missing. Well, it is no good looking towards me for the missing mugs, I haven't time to think let alone brew up. There are only so many hours in a day for logging on to interminably slow computers or mopping up school bags for the hydrophilic that could, if not dealt with promptly, provide reptilian refuge.

Deputy headteacher Don, neither lost nor found – although suspended animation could be highly recommended – has put out some useful information and advice concerning safeguarding. He has written a newsletter regarding online safety and I quote: 'head lice via gangs, volunteers and lanyards'.

I could have done with this pearl of wisdom a few years ago when I was once asked, in a PSE lesson, if pubic lice had the ability to crawl from the 'nether regions' to the armpits. I didn't realise at the time that lice could leg it up a lanyard, negating the need for crampons, but I won't be stumped next time.

Lanyards, it transpires, have other hidden threats, and not just from those that do not scrub their necks to the pinkness my mother liked to achieve. It has come to light that lanyards are being returned to the reception office window at the end of the school day and left outside the window, in a little heap, for any passing Tom, Dick or Harry to help themselves to. But don't worry; because now I know the lanyards are infested, I will have my eye out for any dubious visitors wandering around school scratching their heads.

As I lament my loss to the Police Service, I need to brace myself for the 'rolling a condom onto the model penis' lesson (the art department leads a sheltered life). I do not need my reading glasses to see that specimen looming larger than an alligator pencil case. It could have my eye out and provides proof, if ever proof were needed, that technical and scale drawing should be reintroduced into the curriculum. I will let you know how I get on, with or without the aid of a small pair of yellow fibreglass steps, in my next correspondence.

If there are any more pressing announcements in the 'lost and found', breaking news on nits joining gangs, mugshots of illegal stamps or most urgent appeals for bratwurst machines, you will be the first to know.

So, take great care, and don't beat yourself up over the lifestyle choices you have made, when it turns out that we have all been breathing fetid air for many, many years.

Yours truly

Beth

Feeling Blue

12.02.17

Dear Cassie,

Can you believe it; I have been left holding the baby for a tour of duty in Child Development, a GCSE course that covers the period of a child's life immediately after the contraception lessons have failed but before the child obesity and the healthy eating lessons begin in earnest, unless it is a real bruiser. It is an all-female affair. A male did slip through the net a couple of years ago, upsetting the apple cart and classroom dynamics, but that breach has been secured, a man being the last thing you need under the feet when giving birth, trust me.

During the delivery, to the Year 10 and Year 11 girls, as much attention is given to keeping babies fed and hydrated as is given to the hydration of the school governors, although not necessarily via the same route.

The girls were asked to consider the merits of breastfeeding over bottle feeding and their answers made for some interesting reading, despite a paucity of words to give full and meaningful sentences. I thought you might like to share their words of wisdom; perchance you ever find yourself down to the last can of Nestle Carnation.

'It is more hygienic because it doesn't roll over a dirty floor.'

I presume that is the bosom and not the bottle being given the five-star hygiene rating, although one can never be sure what goes on behind closed doors. However, considering new evidence as to where a lanyard may be looped, and the germs and infestations it may harbour, it is a hygiene rating that could be facing a considerable downgrading.

Learning how to do an evaluation in RPSE and consider all sides of the argument has finally (I never thought the day would come) found a use in the case of nipple versus teat.

'It is easier to carry round with you and a ready-made meal.'

'What is?' Although, quite frankly, anything that avoids spillage trails down the school corridor and an end to slicing and dicing three weeks in advance must be championed, despite excoriation of the ready-made meal from a certain quarter.

'It doesn't go off if left out in a warm room.'

Now there speaks the undeniable confidence of youth, bolstered by the ability to pass the pencil test. The pencil test I hear you ask? Yes, the pencil test, available to anyone bar the mathematical community.

I can distinctly remember, as a teenager, listening to my mother's friend explaining to her the rules of the test. Place a pencil under the bosom and if it immediately drops to the floor – the pencil not the bosom – everything is still looking pert. If not, well, let us just say that this could be a hitherto unexamined route by which the 'more prized than gold' gold and silver metallic marker pens have been illegally leaving the art room. Don't look at me, M'Lord, the answer is not guilty!

'You can get it from the 'tap' whenever the baby needs it.'

I assume – although I should know by now that one should never assume anything in teaching – that the answer should have read, the baby can get breast milk on tap, but prepositions are as scarce as the scale ruler and words in the full sentence.

'Breast milk does not have to cool down and is not too thick or thin, it comes out perfectly.'

Not having to wait for the cooling process would help enormously with timekeeping constraints in the school cooking practical and removing the guilt-ridden choice of should it be healthy semi skimmed, skimmed or water formula for the glugging baby can only be of benefit to the on-trend new mother.

'Breastfeeding is free and helps with bonding.'

I concur, and with current budgetary constraints and the lack of glue sticks, the lactating woman could finally be the answer to all our prayers.

On the reverse side of the argument, the answers that dwelt on cracked and sore nipples, and babies with rock hard gums, are too painful to go into it; besides, as my mother would say, nipples are not a suitable topic of conversation to come up in any learning situation, cracked or otherwise.

'That's not the sort of thing we were taught at the Grammar School' rings resoundingly in my ears almost daily. The lesson was not needed; my mother is an ardent supporter of bottle feeding on the grounds that 'bottle' is an acceptable word and an object that may be viewed, albeit discreetly, in public.

In Personal Social Education, PSE, I have been feeling blue. A strange choice of colour for the model penis and aimed presumably at those that prefer the alfresco approach in mid-January. It's made me think, Cassie, that you could have saved a lot of time and energy over the years, teaching pupils how to carefully blend and mix paints in order to achieve the correct skin tones, when a pot of hyacinth blue would have sufficed.

The standard video to accompany the contraception lesson is called 'Sex in a Shed'. A rather optimistic title when the standard lawn mower barely has room to breathe let alone get up to tricks.

The sixteen stages to 'putting a condom on correctly' (once you've located a condom that is, not the other article – I'm more influenced by my mother's terminology than I like to think) cut and stick exercise seems to be on hold, presumably with the tight rein on glue, photocopying and scissor stocks. I never considered it a necessary exercise for the girls in the first place, who need to be emboldened to say, with conviction, 'that is your job'.

When it came to the class practical element there was the usual resistance from the 'vegetarian' types that can't share a room with any form of rubber, animal or vegetable, a dire lack of tissues to wipe one's hands on afterwards, and a recall count harder to keep a tally of than scoring in a game of rounders.

When asked, 'How far away from your partner should the condom be slipped off?' I thought I showed great restraint by managing not to say, 'Six doors down'. I genuinely believe that there are some areas of life, with my mother's blessing, that pupils should have to work out for themselves, without the supply teacher having to second guess.

On the home front I have also been found wanting. I have been duly scolded by my mother for sending my sister-in-law's birthday card three days late, confusing the 26th January for the 29th January. My mother did not know how it was possible to make such a mistake when the birthday always, indeed 'absolutely always', follows Burns Night. I will have to remember the Rabbie Burns (no it's not a typing error, it is Rabbie as opposed to Robbie as in Williams) method for getting pupils to learn anything with a factual basis in the future when I have learnt when Burns Night is. Clearly knowing that the Clean Air Act was passed in 1956, without recourse to Google, my previous correspondence, is simply not impressive enough for some. If I wasn't so fixated on a condom count, or repeatedly washing my hands – hubby is still complaining that I 'smell funny' (it's not me with the paranoia) – I'd have more time on my hands to concentrate on literary figures. Or so you would think; but expertly rolling out condoms for a living is preferable to the teaching of English Literature. At least I provide the condoms and the model to showcase them; the English department provides neither spare poetry anthologies (for all those who have intentionally lost them), nor the model answer.

Studying poetry, where the hidden meaning of the poem is buried so deeply that no bugger in the classroom can find it, is not a pleasant way to while away the afternoon. A few clues wouldn't go amiss, but the English teachers are as furtive as the poems they are studying and are only prepared, as they nonchalantly walk away from the supply teacher, to give the instruction, 'they know what they are doing'. This translates as, the pupils have as much chance of success as 'rolling on a condom' without puncture, wrinkle, or inappropriate inflation. The English department needs to take a leaf out of the Maths department book, especially if it is from the answer book; or look towards the PSE department, where the objective stares one in the face.

In miscellaneous school news, a second scam has come to light in terms of pupils rewarding themselves with stamps and good comments. A suspicious looking behaviour report card has been handed in to the head of Year 8, with remarkably similar handwriting in the 'comments section' of each lesson, but no teacher signature. Photographic evidence has been supplied, more brownie points for the technologically skilled. Teachers have been asked to put their hand up if one of them has inadvertently filled in every section with the word 'grate', or whether a darker force has been at work. Suffice to say, the owner of the report card has been put on another 'report', ostensibly to work on their forgery skills and spelling for next time.

Another pupil, who has not been turning up to lessons, has been put on report to check their timekeeping and attendance. This approach, presumably, is to keep a clean sheet.

The small, yellow fibreglass step ladders are still proving elusive, but the props provided to Mr Honeyman, aka Props Honeypots, for the 'Alice in Wonderland' production have been put to good use.

A second pupil in your form (no locker issues but dissatisfaction with the Real McCoy) has told me that he is missing you on the grounds that 'the guy' is too old and not

Miss'. Glad the observational drawing skills are finally paying off, although if 'the guy' is older than Methuselah, Cassie, there's not much point in making a hasty dash back. I haven't seen the person in question so cannot comment where on the scale of twenty-three to sixty-three he falls; however, I do have some sympathy and allegiance for fellow supply teachers who lack popularity from all sides. The cheer for the 'substitute' never gets further than the football field.

My heart sinks every time a pupil disparagingly asks me, 'Am I having you today?' Having me in what sense I am never quite sure, but blame the lack of clarity on the declining use of the full sentence. I also have sympathy for those aged before their time but from the Child Development perspective, I am now aware of miracle moisturisers, for specific body parts, that might be helpful in reversing signs of desiccation, borne from the stress of wondering who is 'having you' today, if used sparingly elsewhere in the body.

Please remember that I am your man (or woman or possibly a bit of both these days) for absolutely anything you may need, except for cooking, breastfeeding, contraception, mathematical problems – unless you own your own compass, calculator, and protractor outright – and the life, works and preferred party dates of the Romantic Poets from the late eighteenth century.

Yours truly

Beth

Foaming at the Mouth

06.03.17

Dear Cassie,

Hubby is in a blue funk because he has had to renew his USA visa application, a year before it lapses, due to having a new passport with a new number, and now Donald (Trump not Deputy Don to avoid ambiguity) has left him in 'pending' before a decision is reached.

I'm good to go and Stu says, I thought a tad tetchily, he hopes that I enjoy sitting in the Hertz car rental bay of Philadelphia airport for three weeks.

At least I will be able to have the engine idling. Last year we wasted two hours going over a rental car with a fine-tooth nit comb, looking for the ignition keys, and any previous occupants' diseased stray lanyards, before realising the car was started by the press of a button. Finally, a technological development I approve of. I get so tired of reading e-mails about lost keys with boastful owners who cite their key rings as having tags such as 'greatest teacher' or 'you're the best' for identifying features. And that is just the key rings; missing mugs can accommodate 'the best teacher in the world' signage.

I will, however, be more observant this time when inadvertently pressing buttons on an unfamiliar dashboard. In New Mexico, Stuart said that he didn't appreciate the heated car seat when his arse was already on fire; luckily for him I didn't find the ejector button. It's not only teenagers that can display ingratitude.

Alas, I will not be declaring my hobby at US customs this year, having learnt my lesson the hard way. Last year, when crossing the border back to the US, from a day's excursion to Campobello Island, the holiday home of Roosevelt in New Brunswick, Canada, the border guard asked if we were bringing back any cigarettes, liquor, or arms. I politely replied only postcards and before we knew it, we got the terse order to 'Spring the trunk, cut the engine and get out of the vehicle'.

Some people have no sense of humour. If Stuart had been able to cut the engine a little bit quicker and hit the button, rather than reaching for non existent keys, he might not be in 'pending' right now. Using the defence, 'I'm in a sauna and can't see,' won't thaw the ice with the Americans (I'm still taking every opportunity to luxuriate with the heated car seat in conjunction with the air conditioning, putting into practice the school mantra of make the best of the options available to you).

Our son Alex, a conspiracy theorist, says his dad is on hold because 'they' – whoever they may be – know everything about 'you' and we will be on a watch list. Well, in that case, 'they' should know I am a profoundly serious postcard collector, although due to the demands of the school day, I have never had time to share this with you.

Not all family members share my passion for deltiology. My daughter refers to my lifelong hobby as an addiction, my son as future kindling and Stuart is already espousing warning noises about 'limits' this year due to plunging exchange rates. I don't suppose any of them will be having a whip round, any time soon, for the 'greatest deltiologist' mug.

Mugs, as it happens, are one of the supply teacher's daily hazards. If people wish to live with more microbes than found on the average breastfeeding mother wearing a lanyard that is their choice, but school is a communal space and I do not wish to share their germs.

The science department devotes a lot of lessons to culturing bacteria on agar plates, to give credence to the fact that microbes exist – a waste of precious resources, when a school tour of the average classroom teacher's desk could show nature in action. It's truly obscene, although I'll get on to the mug belonging to the school housekeeper, Mrs Braithwaite, for different reasons in a minute.

It is not just the stained, chipped, cracked, furry mugs, so filthy that the word 'Governor' barely shows, but the rotting, rank detritus left on misappropriated plates. I have perfected opening school doors with a kick of the foot, to avoid ever having to touch a handle, but have lost the ability (too many Florentines) and an arthritic hip to swing my leg up on to the desk to cast the offending articles out of the way.

Light switches are another bone of contention and need treating with caution on two fronts: the biological hazard, and the eco setting – where you can't see the light of day, but behavioural incidents are less likely to be reported. Ignorance is bliss.

In the past, flicking a light switch was a two-choice option, and with a bottle of hand gel at the ready, well within my capabilities. But now, the switch has been replaced by a touch screen pad, offering more combinations than the school contraceptive box, with typography so small that the lights need to be on to get started.

Racy Mrs Braithwaite's mug is of special scientific interest for many reasons. Rather than trumpeting the 'greatest whatever', the mug stands proud because it has a picture on the front of it. Admittedly, not in the style of Constable, but nonetheless, a very arresting scene, or it would be if a constable were on site. The image on the front, of a man, alters depending upon whether the mug contains a hot or cold drink. Let us just say that when the mug contains a hot drink something rises on the image that would make a PSE teacher blush. I once borrowed it and was halfway down the school corridor before I realised what a hot potato I had in my hands and, as a result, have the burn marks to prove it. Hardly the sort of visual aid we need in school for promoting the use of scientific smart materials.

The e-mails this week, Cassie, have not been very inspiring with endless bragging about who has lost or found the largest fob. However, I have noticed a surge in those playing 'break time duty swap shop', with lots of incentives and sweeteners being given such as 'you can come in from the cold'.

The design and technology department has had some sort of incident over a pile of wood and foam being dumped in the woodwork room. I can see how this could generate a crisis when they usurped wood for the benefits of acrylic many years ago. I have not been able to work out, yet, whether it is the presence of the wood, or the foam, that has given the offence, but the matter is being investigated very seriously.

No information has been released as to the nature of the foam, (various options exist, solid sheeting, 'stuffing' as used for stuffing gonks, now known as puglies with the fetish for upmarket rebranding or shaving foam). However, Mr Honeyman has been charged with the task of clearing up, so that sounds suspiciously to me like the incident could be linked to the production of 'Alice in Wonderland', and an after-production dismantling exercise gone wrong. I really am more suited to the role of school detective than general supply teacher. I am surprised this infringement escaped a certain eagled eyed presence in another wing of the design and technology department where a microbe can't sit back, put its feet up, and relax on a surgically disinfected tabletop, let alone a plank of wood embellished with foam.

The photocopying machine, in the optimistically named 'resource department', continues to break down every other day with increasing regularity; however, with less demand for certificates honouring the act of breathing there should be slack in the system. Suspiciously though, I am beginning to wonder if 'we are waiting for the engineer' is code for reducing photocopying costs via the back door. I might not be able to see the modern-day light switch, but you can't fool me with 'the staff copier is currently jamming during double sided copying, so use single sided copying only'. It is the thin end of the wedge, surely?

And when one starts they all start (the coughing symphony) because the blue minibus has unceremoniously ground to a halt (gear box trouble). Minibus Marlene, regular bundle of cheer, bursar and controller of all school wheels is not amused. Rather than sending messages to say that the blue minibus, or even more delipidated maroon minibus, for that matter, is off the road, why doesn't the school release, in advance, the few days a year when it can cough up the petrol money to have the fuel tanks stocked and the minibuses running?

The science department is taking children (by last minute hired coach) to a lecture on 'science live' which will make a refreshing change from their usual torpid state.

The staff daily bulletin, on the other hand, continues to induce the torpidity the science department is trying so desperately hard to reverse and notice should be given to those collecting notices for the bulletin (that would be the two ladies that man the 'resourceless department'), 'by the end of the day please', that we don't need reminding, every single, unremitting day, of their duties when we have our own duties to attend.

Excitingly, before I finish my letter to you, another e-mail has pinged into my 'in box', to say that the self-appointed CEO of the school exchange and mart, Mr Honeyman, has a pile of decent quality upholstery foam.

'Curiouser and curiouser,' cried Alice, attributable to Lewis Carroll, not Honeypots – I do not want my mother or anyone else thinking my literary knowledge is wanting. Apparently, he has enough foam to fill a small shed and suggests, 'any

DIY, home improvements, customised pet beds, new caravan /or boat cushions and the like'.

I can think of a few things that need stuffing but politeness and an upbringing where self expression was frowned upon prevent me from saying. No mention was given to surplus wood for boat building purposes to place your newly sprung boat cushions, but I live in hope.

What is needed is a cushion making sale to help boost school funds, to get the wagon wheels rolling, and provide a luxurious foam padded classroom to hurl oneself against at the end of the school day.

As always, it goes without saying, Cassie, I am thinking of you, and if you want to carry out some arts and crafts for therapeutic purposes, I know just the man to see. You are also welcome to browse through my postcard collection at any time to help with relaxation techniques and if you are game, the school chicken lady is looking for volunteers for the chicken feeding rota. Alternatively, if you would prefer to sit with your feet up, with a mug of hot cocoa, I will see if the housekeeper's mug is available to you. It could be an icebreaker when you have got visitors and you are keen to divert their attention from the usual deliberation, speculation, investigation, medication, and evaluation of your ongoing situation.

Yours truly

Beth

Donkey Work

30.03.17

Dear Cassie,

The loan of the risqué mug was never intended for use with the octogenarian visitor; I'm not surprised you've had spillages. That kind of shock could have led to mouth to mouth, perish the thought. 'Not firing on all cylinders' is absolutely no excuse; the pupils know better. In future, follow the pupils' lead (they are experts in the field), and commit to memory, beforehand, a convincing line from the standard reference on the topic 'The Mother of all Excuses'.

One person who is firing on all cylinders is a fresh-faced teaching assistant to the school – male, late twenties, hyperactive, tendency to run on the spot and with a propensity to inappropriately shout out (namely when I am speaking to the hitherto settled class), 'I'm cooking on gas'. A stint in the food technology department, when the diminutive key for the gas box that controls the gas (a mixture of hydrocarbons, predominantly methane, molecular formula CH_4, chemical structure one carbon atom covalently bonded to four hydrogen atoms – put that in your pipe and smoke it, Mrs Prendergast), to the cookers is lost, should cure him of that.

Methinks cooking on carbon dioxide only, critical readings rocketing with every exercising step.

On the home front, I have finally got some good news (no need for fanfare, star jumps or the merits of the camping stove) to impart. Daughter Meg has got her long-held wish of joining the boys in blue.

It is not PC to say WPC anymore, to be politically correct; we must adhere to PC Meg, although, if it involves a child she will be known as PC Megsy, less intimidating to the child when she bangs them up. (We should be so lucky.) I am not at liberty to divulge any information gleaned so far, but suffice to say, there is a lot more urination in public going on than meets the eye, unless, that is, the culprits have really perfected their aim.

My mother's response to Meg's choice of career was, 'I don't think much to the garb.' Well, I blame the Scouts. If Meg hadn't trailed after her older brother to 'Cubs and Scouts' instead of following the usual 'Brownies and Guides' route for girls, she would never have got such a liking for the all-encompassing belt. I've suggested she dangles a few spare bottles from it to make use of all the public urination – it is an essential ingredient for damn fine compost making, especially if from a male (something to do with superior hormones, but don't broadcast that) – and it would give Stuart a break, as in winter, he is constantly complaining of the cold.

Meg says that as an apartment dweller (she is quite touchy about the word flat) she has no interest whatsoever in the ingredients needed to make sublime compost and, in light of her new role, I ought to be giving more consideration to her father's indecent exposure than perfecting its crumbly texture. In response, I have made clear that she will never know true satisfaction in life until she has produced the perfect compost and that our compost bin is nothing if not discreetly placed.

The new recruit's mode of transport, the panda car, must be devoid of the heated car seat, or the mini hot composter, because we have been asked to stump up for thermal vests. Running after the criminals (aerobically for the saunter, anaerobic respiration for the sprint – stitch not looking likely), to generate a bit of heat, is clearly expecting too much. Then again, the new police boot (basics not wanted, designer range only, guess who is footing the bill?) does take some mastery, especially for the slender, but extra-long foot.

The advice given for the special boot fitting ceremony – 'curl the toes tightly' (a snug size seven is so much more ladylike than the small male size eight) – was met with derision. Furthermore, instead of admiration for 'two heads are better than one', my mother and I were read our Rights (not so much 'you have the right to remain silent', as 'you will stay silent') and told, in no uncertain terms, that until we could find the strength to lift the police vest, either singularly or combined, to kindly butt out. Moreover, it was ridiculous of us to think, in the present-day era, that having a foot in the style of Thumper was going to be an impediment to tripping down the aisle.

I am so deflated on the marriage – or lack of it – front that I can barely get excited over my second piece of good news (one small jig and a hip hip hooray as much as I can muster).

Hubby has finally been granted visa entry for the USA. I'm not surprised it has been a lengthy process and that the authorities were suspicious of his travel plans. How many people, do you think, fly to Philadelphia airport, to then declare their first night's stay is in Washington? It is akin to flying to Edinburgh for a holiday in London but that is the snag of the bargain flight. It's precisely this sort of covert behaviour that has led Alex to his assertion 'you are both barking' (rather unfair on the tag along passenger) although not as barking as next door's dog in the middle of his packing.

Our next-door neighbour's son's dog, Paddy (an Irish wolfhound in case you are puzzling – not much scope for the imaginative naming), is going to America for a wedding, as his master is getting married out there – to an American that is, not to Paddy, although with so many partner combinations these days it's always best to clarify. Evidently, the Irishman has achieved travel clearance quicker than hubby has, probably because Paddy could remember his vaccination history more clearly. Had I known that dogs needed their own passport for travel, I would have supplied Stuart with a handy pack of anti-bacterial wipes for the photo booth. A drooling dog with a hairy paw adjusting the photo stool is enough to put one off foreign travel.

Anyway, by all accounts, especially the financial (I've had it from the horse's mouth, thank god not Paddy's) it is very expensive to fly a dog transatlantic when there's no paddy wagon available, and the mutt doesn't get so much as a window seat, or a bag of nuts, thrown in for its troubles (APTA and muzzle protected). Surprisingly, it is the responsibility of the passenger's owner to supply the food and cage. Well, that is a relief. I do not want some great big shaggy beast lolling on me, Cassie (even if it is your idea of heaven) for the duration of the flight, staring the salted snacks out of my hand.

I am not a dog lover at any time (unmitigated fear) and dislike the owners even more ('sorry' clearly the hardest word, offers for the dry-cleaning bill to neutralise the slobber never forthcoming).

Moreover, why do the 'canine besotted' make inane comments such as 'the lady is unsure' or 'the lady doesn't want to talk' when the lady is cocksure that she neither wants to converse with or have a mongrel within a hundred feet. The dog may be curious, another line I am frequently subjected to, but considering where the fiend may previously have poked its nose (despicable social habits), I have no curiosity whatsoever.

On top of that, I have no time for the exasperating, extendable dog lead. I thought the idea was for the owner to have control, not a dog with nous weighing up the benefits of running rings around their master, or legging it, immune to calls of 'come back here'.

Please don't think that I'm singling out and 'picking' on pooches in particular (adolescent speak rubs off so easily) because my dislike extends to anything winged, finned, or furry, fang group milk, permanent or false.

To put it mildly, I am not an animal person. The Blackpool donkey (happy childhood days) is the sole exception. And now, even the beloved donkey has had its image tainted following my latest eye-opening contraception lesson, this time featuring the 'femidom', a female condom, two words that should never be put side by side. (Or God forbid, inside.)

The only good thing I can say about the lesson (clutching at straws) is that the 'hot lips pink for girls' model vagina didn't have to be dragged out for demonstration purposes. Which is just as well because there was so much yardage to the 'thing' (dermatitis flaring with every hand scrubbing) that without resorting to hospital corners (mother's influence again) I can't think how it would all have tucked in.

I barely knew where to look when a boy with a prurient interest in the topic, combined with an ability to think outside of the box, commented 'Is that thing meant for a donkey, Miss?' I did think the item more suited to the ass than the human, but could hardly concur for fear of launching 'cooking on gas' man and an excitable class into outer orbit. Someone in the classroom must remain the voice of reason. And if you are wondering what has become of my small, furry 'Spanish donkey with sombrero' holiday memento for the key ring, don't worry, it has been surreptitiously replaced by an enamelled Minnie Mouse. No need for further asinine visual aids to prompt untoward questioning when dampening, not inciting, the mood of a braying crowd.

Talking of key rings and keys, I couldn't make it up if I wanted to, a bunch of keys has been left in the resource department – flowery strap saying 'you are what you eat, avoid fruit and nuts'. Whatever happened to greetings from Great Yarmouth? Alex is right about 'them' (the shadowy group) knowing everything about 'you', when even key rings can carry an implicit threat. Don't you just long for the guilt-free days of the nineteen eighties, when you could munch a toffee crisp without furring the arteries, cracking the hip, or having the heavy-handed key mob rattling the lock to serve a 'final warning'.

The resource ladies are not complaining though, because in addition to collecting keys and key rings as a hobby (diminutive gas box key missing from the collection), they have been entertaining the engineer for days and days and even more days on end, with the result that they now have two fully functioning photocopying machines. They have heralded this miracle with the message, 'All who have requested photocopying need to form an orderly queue as we are completely snowed under.' That's one way of putting it! Have you noticed how there are certain school groups (and the award goes to the caretakers), that never miss a trick to let other people know how much work they get through in a day (inversely proportional to the amount of work achieved), but at least the resource ladies are in the right place to reward themselves with the self congratulatory certificate.

The forgery business, not a photocopy in sight, is up and running. Miss Moorhouse, Business Studies teacher, and according to the pupils, 'Miss More Arse' than anyone else, has announced that if there is a note in any Year 9 pupil planner to leave lessons early it must be IGNORED. A fellow form member has been providing the early bird service and has perfected her signature.

Mr Honeyman is trying to track down a (YPO) Yorkshire Purchasing Order delivery that has gone astray containing three adhesive spray cans and five craft knives, originally intended for 'Alice'. He'll be lucky.

A solution has been put forward for the unsafe visitor wandering around school scratching their head. A lockable post box for green lanyards (the colour denoting someone has been DBS checked, Disclosure and Barring Service), is to be provided and the lanyards must be returned personally by anyone who has had a visitor for the day, engineers included. I don't know what materials Mr Honeyman will be constructing the lockable box out of, as yet, but I am sure he will be putting out an announcement any day soon for spares. Last year's request for a small chicken run – not the animated film but an actual run /pen/ coop – along with his ardent desire for peacock feathers may finally have found a use.

I'd keep my eye out, on his behalf, if I wasn't focusing on the fruits of my autumn labour, the emergence of over one thousand, glorious, and tastefully colour-blended (brazen reds and flamboyant oranges barred) tulip bulbs. I've made it clear to the less floriferous appreciating family members (spouse and offspring alike), that when looking out onto a sea of wondrous nodding pastels, 'it's no-good counting individuals; you have to view the show as a whole'.

Alex, a chef, likes to labour that I don't grow anything useful, but that would depend on what your view of useful is. His supposedly reassuring fact that a coconut landing on the noggin is more harmful than smoking cannabis does not make me want to lend him a bag of compost, even the connoisseur homemade variety, anytime soon.

The WPC minus the W has an apartment with a balcony that looks onto concrete and tarmac that, curiously, is more aesthetically pleasing to her eye than my display. Stuart, meanwhile, fazed by the show, is on a recount. I can't see the problem; I'm not going for professional help (although another pair of hands would come in mightily handy at planting time) until collecting postcards and Dutch tulip bulbs have made it on to the PSE syllabus, under the heading of the 'deadliest of addictions'.

I hope that you are enjoying somewhat tamer hobbies (bungee jumping would cause less of a headache) and making the most of the time spent away from school to help your recuperation. Time and tide wait for no man, Cassie, so galvanise into action, and devise a plan. The methodical, over the slapdash (a slap of paint here, a slap of paint there, let's slosh it everywhere) arty approach, always produces better results. You are too late for the tulip plantings, but joy of joys: there are always gladioli and lilies to fall back upon, should you be overcome with the urge.

Yours truly,

Beth

Not in the Pink

07.04.17

Dear Cassie,

Tracking down who has intercepted the (YPO) Yorkshire Purchasing Order box of three spray can adhesives and five craft knives is still ongoing, but word on the street is that art should be put in the frame.

If it is an art insider job, don't worry unduly; at least you've got a semi decent excuse, and one certainly a notch up from the overused 'PE kit is in the wash' line. How many PE kits can be trapped on low temperature eco mode, no time for the spin, by the formidable childproof lock? It could provide the basis for a thought-provoking philosophy essay, 'Machines rule PE'. Discuss.

The cynical mind might think that the regulation school shoe is also finding the rinse mode. Lack of coordination with the ubiquitous water bottle or the fluidly fluid fruit fusion is not the 'sole' reason given (more perforations than a tea bag) for the soggy sock, necessitating the need for the wearing of trainers, the podiatrist's answer to all that ails the foot. More drenched shoes than puddles kicking about. The 'writing hand' as injury prone as the stubbed toe in a downpour, also has issues, gripping issues when it comes to mobile phone and water bottle release.

In other news, there has been a surfeit of photocopying collections heading to the wrong departments. Imagine pupils' disappointment, sitting down to do a test on 'Sex and Contraception' and being given a French letter looking for a host on the French exchange instead. It could have been worse: the modern foreign language department has been handing out Chinese letters – hope they are up to snuff and not a cheap imitation. The department has obviously got the wind up since the panic buying of pasta machines and decided to look to the Orient for inspiration, but as most pupils find the learning of languages 'Chinese' in the first place, there's no need to change the pupils' language learning habits of a lifetime.

As for other problems arising from the cross-curricular photocopying interchange (I can do jargon with the best of them), I am not overly concerned. It will not be long before exchange and mart man, Mr Honeyman, senses a niche in the market and establishes a thriving trade in photocopying swaps before it can be said, 'Who has gone off with my original?'.

In the latest addition to their burgeoning silverware collection, the resource department has reported a silver key ring with lots of keys but no fob, on the guillotine. Rather a harsh decision but clearly the resource department has not been schooled in the restorative approach to behaviour if they are going straight for the chop. For the sake of the evaluation, it could be, of course, that the keys have flung themselves at the guillotine deliberately, at the shame of being fob less, neither belonging to the greatest teacher in the world nor being charged with the responsibility of giving out life saving food allergy warnings.

The blue minibus is back on the road but anyone failing to take responsibility to stock the fuel tank, under Minibus Marlene's instruction, will also be for the chopping block and I wouldn't want to be the one to challenge that decision. It doesn't look good to the general public if the pupils are sitting on the verge, flicking the Vs at passing motorists, when the fuel has run out mid-journey, even if it does help with global emissions following geography's code for the sustainable environment.

Big Mac is providing cakes in the staff room at morning break time, not for the return of the small, yellow fibreglass step ladders – bunting will be put out for that one, once the school knitting club has swung into action – but in celebration of his 'big' birthday. Glory be. I hope he has an EpiPen on standby for the nut, egg, wheat, milk, gluten, muffin, and latex allergy sufferers, since it has come to light, following my contraception lesson, that touching, let alone eating certain objects, can induce hives.

Planners, coats, and gym bags continue to wander through the ether, shockingly unaccompanied, giving Deputy Don further headache, with urgent requests and a sweep of the school to find them. If only the owners could take responsibility and retrace their own steps, to jog the memory, without feeling the need to 'share' and clutter up my 'in box'. Although jogging the memory is not all it is cracked up to be. When I was on jury service a few years ago – can't divulge details of the case for fear of ending up in the Tower, and I don't mean the school tower block housing the Hair and Beauty Salon, once the sole preserve of the technical college, now the showpiece of the school (more severed heads sporting hacked wigs, in a bid to perfect the gruesome) – but suffice to say, accurate translation is key. Apparently, 'let me jog your memory' and 'does this ring a bell' have a completely different meaning in Urdu.

What is not lost in translation, 'Geordie' the exception, whether speaking Urdu, Mongolian, or Cantonese (the Chinese menu never a last resort – all monosodium glutamate, no Yorkshire pudding), is that my husband requires his tea on the dot of five, no leeway for added travel time, court delay or jury deliberation. The 5.25 (evening meal, not King's Cross to Wakefield) is unacceptable to a man hyperventilating, but we can't all subscribe to the 'bring it on, ready or not' salmonella school of cooking, simply to counter the effects of the panic attack.

Meg, the calmest family member, was more relaxed – not a paper bag in sight – about the later dining arrangements at the time. Not that her tummy wasn't rumbling with the best of them, but she felt that she could ask her best buddy, and daughter of one of the school governors, for tea without 'bud' looking green around the gills at the family dinner table. Five twenty-five was marginally nearer to the friend's 'normal' eating hour of eight o'clock (commonly known as bedtime in households steeped in 'early to bed, early to rise'), allowing buddy to make 'slightly more room' due to the belated timing.

My mother, 'Delicate Stomach' – a medical condition not the name of a Native American squaw – has a morbid fear of eating at an 'unearthly hour'. Such depravity only leads to the meal resting heavily on, rather than lightly within, the delicate (not cast iron) organ in question and she has successfully passed her phobia on to my husband, but it's not the kind of phobia you hear regularly discussed on Radio Four's 'In the Psychiatrist's Chair'.

Alex has never been interested in being more like a 'normal' family, only in having a 'normal' mother – make of that what you will – and the pupils frequently bemoan that they want the 'normal' teacher. It is a very heavy cross to bear but nothing compared to the challenge of standing upright, after eating stew and dense dumplings (undercooked), to meet last orders.

On the teaching front I have had the misfortune to spend yet another torrid day in the soul-destroying maths department. The French irreverent teatime holds out more hope for survival than working in the insidious culture of unruliness that can be a feature of the substitute maths lesson-backup, and increasingly the work needed for the lesson, nonexistent. Mr Fitzsimmons would be better named Mr Findlater. I need the textbooks, the graph paper, and the nail varnish remover at the start of the lesson, not at the end when the riot has subsided.

What is more, I am completely out of date with the modern-day mathematical mnemonic. In my day, the trigonometry rules 'Sine Opposite Hypotenuse', 'Cosine Adjacent Hypotenuse', and 'Tangent Opposite Angle' were remembered by SOH, CAH, TOA.

So, I nearly fell off the chair with more clatter and disturbance than the average attention-seeking child, honing their skills for drama approval, when I was informed that the memory, from a mnemonic doing the rounds on the internet, could be stimulated in other ways.

Sex On Hard surfaces Can Always Hurt The Orgasmic Areas. Is nothing sacred? If pupils followed my mother's guidance of sex in a bed, not the kitchen table, after marriage, with the windows firmly closed, they would not need to worry about friction burns. Science will be jumping in on the act next to help with their friction explanation, although looking at the combined age of the science department they have probably forgotten what friction is. And PSE must be smarting that another department has stolen its thunder. Although to stymie parental complaint, the maths department did quickly ban the use of the mnemonic, as soon as it was made aware of its existence, in a bid to prevent pupils going off at a wrong tangent.

To keep out of stressful mathematical situations I have decided to pursue less onerous teaching avenues such as the teaching of Mandarin Chinese or perfecting the batch method of soup making. Even better would be a period of history, any period that did not involve 'soilders' or 'sholders', too much toll on the marking hand. It is not as if a child ever gets to see their corrections, not when by school law they are made in green ink one shade up from the invisible.

Changing the subject, in more ways than one, Stuart and I are going away for the weekend, leaving West Yorkshire, to visit my sister and her family in North Yorkshire. I will be taking plenty of snacks because headteachers (she is one) are out of the same mould as school governors when it comes to the 'civilised eating hour'. You wouldn't believe we share the same mother. My mother had got lax when it came to the last.

And the differences do not stop with the 'civilised eating hour' (some of us more civilised and diurnal than others) – we share different tastes in colour schemes. I only bring this to your attention, Cassie, because you are a colour expert and I would value your thoughts on one of her more dastardly (never as dastardly as brother – ink on his hands, doll's face never recovered) sisterly acts.

As children we shared a bedroom that was painted, by prerogative of birth, in soft candy pink. Upon leaving home for college and following my first visit home after a month's banishment (the words 'you may come home sooner if feeling unsettled' never murmured), I returned to find the bedroom painted in 'Habitat Green', a habitat suited only to the needs of the visiting Leprechaun, or hesitant dining guest placed on first sitting. Furthermore, my treasured collections – costume dolls, shells, bookmarks, rocks and fossils, twelve petite china figurines (representing each month of the year), Nancy Drews and the earlier postcard albums (special areas of interest Bridlington, Filey and Hornsea – my mother was collecting the pottery at the time, building up a full dinner service piecemeal), all boxed up, with a note: 'you've got a problem and I need the room'.

Eighteen years of my life pressed into a bundle under new bedroom rule. 'The King is dead. Long live the King!'

It is a cautionary tale to tell but one you would be wise to remember; the 'take no mementos' attitude is essential if you wish to gain power at the top of the school.

However, with changing times, I suspect my sister may live to rue the day she ever threw out my lovely, coordinated soft candy pink candlewick bedspread (still attached to the bed – a defining moment) in the fight for space now that the European continental quilt has had the stuffing knocked out of its system. Which reminds me, have you given any thought to taking up patchwork quilting with wadding? I believe the handmade quilt is making quite a comeback. No need for the 'too clever for its own good' sewing machine going down the wrong seam. Artisan products are all the rage these days.

As for my brother (you really have to have had one to fully understand), I barely know where to begin, although 'my brother and the teenage ferret years' would be as good a place to start as any. When I say brother and the teenage ferret years (brother the teenager, not the ferret), I am referring to my common bond with the presenter Richard Whiteley, not painting a bedroom with a five litre can of matt emulsion in 'ferret with a hint of musk'. Have you seen the names of the Farrow and Ball paints my sister now favours since emerging from a habitat not known for casting a rosy glow to the complexion – Mouse's Back, Dead Salmon, Mole's Breath, Great White? It's not natural, although having to capture such bizarre creature ingredients probably goes someway to justifying the exorbitant prices. A tin of 'Candy Pink' never rocked the boat. If it had, I would have been asked to crush up some fallen pink rose petals in a free transparent liquid to slap on the walls.

I suggest checking your own watercolour set, Cassie, to make sure the lapis lazuli hasn't been replaced with 'le soufflé du lapin' (for the sake of accurate translation – rabbit's breath, not an inedible dessert that the upwardly mobile food technology department is considering marketing).

Yours truly,

Beth

PS In the interest of fair play, brother did train the ferret to bite either sister, no overt favouritism displayed.

A Fish Out of Water

10.05.17

Dear Cassie,

The school receptionist has joined the bandwagon with the following request: 'If anyone has visitor lanyards 'floating' around, please could you return them as soon as possible to reception.' There is a lot more to the lanyard than meets the eye. Well, one will not be needed for Chong, floating or otherwise, because the Mandarin Club has been cancelled due to Chong, the tutor, being ill. Mrs Drinkwater will be desperately trying to reel in the replacement tutor.

The school receptionist, in her secondary role as school tie purveyor, to her credit, continues to 'dress the figures' with ever dwindling borrowed school tie stocks. Big Mac will have her tied up in Windsor knots once he realises the losses from the soft wear section are as high as those from the hardware department.

A male pupil, stretching the rules to the limit – the pinching regulation school shoe, all other forms of footwear perfectly roomy – is wearing trainers, supported by a note from Mum. Wearing the correct shoes in the first place would negate the need for extra support with fallen arches at the later date.

There was no mention in the note of fungal, bacterial, or viral infection requiring the constant sucking of lozenges, throughout the school day, to aid the foot recovery.

Big Mac is angling for a pat on the back as he puts out feelers for arranging 'PAT', portable appliance testing. Nailing the items down would be a start so that they do not go the same way as the small, yellow fibreglass steps with blue holster top (the devil is in the detail). We will never know if the steps had a stable centre of gravity, or not, as they are still unavailable for testing. However, the pupil whose locker key was thrown onto the modern foreign language block roof on Friday afternoon, and is instructed to see Mr Mackenzie at Monday morning registration first thing, is going to be in for a disappointment, or as it is Mac, should I say, big disappointment.

The detention register board has gone missing. This is a matter of grave concern. Letters cannot be sent home to arrange detentions with pupils who, more than likely, already have a prior engagement. The school cannot and must not be held responsible for any double bookings.

My husband has boldly made a booking of his own. He has secured some bargain price Virgin train tickets: ten pounds return, Wakefield to King's Cross. He is not known as coupon man for nothing, although it is his abiding aim.

I haven't been to London for thirty-five years, still smarting at the shame of our last visit. Some things go to the very core. At the time of the capital blunder I was encouraged, as it was our first venture away together, to go for anything I pleased on the menu. Stuart, coupons in hand, was trying to impress and so I tucked in with relish to fillet steak, a rarity that had never featured on one of my mother's standard seven, despite the protein requirements of the ever-growing boy. (On family walks the promise of a Bernie Inn Steak House was often held out as an incentive to complete ten-mile hikes, but always reneged upon due to 'undue falling out and needless moaning' along the way – pandering hadn't caught on in those days.)

So, I made the most of what was on offer, feeling more relaxed than when reclining on the heated car seat in the desert, until, that is, the bill came. Stuart's coupons only entitled him to a discount for items on an extremely limited menu, not the whole shebang, and we did not have the necessary funds to make up the required difference. The mortification was probably the start of my stomach problems, Gaviscon by drip; although there is a distinct possibility the problems are hereditary. Is it any wonder I was tense by the time we got to Earl's Court Arena to see a Supertramp concert, my first and last concert, as it turns out, to see any musical group, super, trouper, or otherwise despite an overriding fondness for Abba.

Stuart did not, and would not, pay any attention to where the fire exits were sited which, according to my upbringing, is the first thing you establish upon entering an unfamiliar building. Furthermore, having to wait until the arena cleared at the end of the concert hardly lightened the mood, but one of us had to take the risk of stampede seriously. The present-day pupil, along with the rest of the world, might have the 'I can't live without a mobile phone' attitude but then, as now,

I can't live without the escape route mapped out.

So, lessons learnt, this time around we perused the art galleries and museums – less damage to the tympanum, and a more sedate pace in the event of an unexpected charge.

Lunch was to be a surprise and it certainly lived up to the task. Strolling past numerous trendy bistros, bars, and cafes on the way to the National Portrait Gallery, I never gave a moment's thought to the gourmet delights of the crypt. The cafe, in the crypt of 'St Martins in the Field', even with the 'bargain basement bribe', was hardly conducive to getting the digestive juices naturally flowing. In fact, I think I'd go as far as to say that we should have been handing them the chit.

The evening meal, at an Italian restaurant called Carluccio's, buy one 'mains' and get a second 'mains' for a pound (goodness only knows what the crypt was offering – buy one mains, and take a body bag home) lived up to its promise. I scrutinise all small print very carefully these days; once caught twice shy, and I don't relish a scene.

Meg commented that she thought we had done an awful lot of eating for the day, but as I explained, by avoiding the tube (a survival must), we had crammed three months' worth of daily steps into twenty-four hours and without adequate fuel, one cannot successfully step.

Meg, as always, asked for a postcard tally count (inheritance worries creeping in again) adding, 'Surely you know what London landmarks look like without having to go for a Big Ben?' I do, but there are an awful lot of pictures in the National Gallery and I wanted mementos of the paintings I had seen. You would have been proud; I managed to spy (the training has not been lost) a postcard of a Rousseau painting depicting a tiger poking about in the long grass. Just the sort of image, Cassie, that you and your fellow art teachers like to admire for months, and in the case when I am teaching art lessons, for months and months and months on end. (The RPSE department has the evaluation and the unanswerable God question to pan lessons out; the art department remains shrouded in camouflage.) I can finally see the attraction: it's all about blending into the natural environment and I'm wondering if stripes could be the answer to my digestive prayers. Clever camouflage and survival stillness are the only means left at my disposal for fooling pupils into not hammering on the locked classroom door at lunchtime.

For the train journey itself I didn't think that we commanded the correct, nonchalant pose. Too busy searching for access points. To look a seasoned train traveller, you need to have a mobile phone in one hand and a Starbucks coffee in the other; shame Starbucks aren't big on offers. For any other unencumbered body parts there was a message on the train wall, next to the seat, which read precisely, word wise and grammatically: 'Power Up. Plug in and grab some juice for your mobile tablet, or laptop. No toasters or hairdryers please'.

Food technology will be delighted at the extent to which the healthy eating message is getting across (they are champions of juice – by the bucket, when all is said and done), although I'm not sure that tablets should be able to roam under their own steam. I suppose we should forgive a Virgin for not knowing where to insert a comma properly. And until travellers can balance a two-slicer, or a four-slicer for those with finishing school training, on the end of the hooter, or the latest 'must have' mobile phone (gee-wizz- well it's something to with the Gs) can smartly curl and dress the tresses, I doubt I'll need to plan my escape route due to burnt toast or singed hair, any time soon.

Knowing where to hit a window to find its greatest point of weakness in an emergency, or how to lower oneself out of a burning building by the fingertips to help lessen the fall, is not the only thing going out of fashion these days.

Meg is less than pleased to find out that not every family, when going away on holiday, put down dust sheets to avoid the carpets fading. I'm of the mind, as is my mother, that if you leave the curtains fully drawn for more than two days running, to keep the soft furnishings in good order, it's an open invitation for the burglars to come on in to feel the plushness of the pile for themselves. Never stint on the underlay.

Apparently, according to Meg's work colleagues at the council, prior to joining the police (she will categorically not be promoting my advice at neighbourhood police training), this is not normal holiday preparation, and she is furious with me for using some sort of 'Pavlovian' technique for making her think that it is 'normal'. When she told her council colleagues that she was packed and ready for departure with only the dust sheets left to put down, her colleagues had stared at her. Evidently, it is a greater social faux pas than having your tea at five o'clock in a carpeted, magnolia-painted kitchen.

Well, wait until she is invited on a date to the crypt and

then she will know the true meaning of a social faux pas!

I think it would be opportune for you to get some dust sheets down of your own, Cassie, and book a holiday in 'less expensive' term time. Do not 'procrastinate' – (Word of the Week) in the daily pupil bulletin – as 'procrastination is the thief of time,' Charles Dickens (Thought of the Week). Take heart that one member of the entire school community has taken heed of the word and thought of the week and wants you to act upon it. A relaxing holiday, and a change of scene, could be just what the doctor ordered.

Yours truly,

Beth

PS What do you mean Candy Pink sounds a little sugary?

Alarm Bells Ringing

19.05.17

Dear Cassie,

Happy Birthday! What can I say, all the best people are born in May, an imminently sensible, and by far the finest month to arrive in the world, joyously coinciding with the burst of spring and early summer blooms, birthday presents in themselves.

I trust you will be making the most of the floral show, especially mine, particularly as a man (still counting) has proclaimed 'enough tulip bulbs to rival Keukenhof!'. Think south west of where 'a little mouse with clogs on' clogged (danced, not popped) and you will be somewhere near the field. (If you cannot beat the quizzers, Mother especially, you may as well join them.) The point is, however, there is so much more to the great outdoors than gingerly hanging out of the window, trying to dissipate the fug, with only a blast of synthetic pine fresh at your disposal. The natural, heady, intoxicating perfumes of summer must be appreciated at first-hand.

So, as you prepare for an unaccustomed rush of oxygen to the head, Cassie, I will endeavour to get you up to date with matters pertaining to school, before our departure to the States, with Donald's blessing of course.

Firstly, great technological advances have been made in your absence. The Head of RPSE has requested that a girl in her form, on crutches, be allowed to leave lessons 'ahead of time' so that she can 'travel' to her next lesson.

Futuristic time travel with the aid of a crutch is not the only development we should be in awe of. The walkie talkies in the school office have gone 'walkie walkies' making them most definitely ahead of their time. However, in the here and now, Minibus Marlene (not a happy bunny) is on the hunt for whoever has had the audacity to unplug the large (what other adjective could it be in the big school setting) coffee machine.

Marlene's not the only one running on empty. Big Mac has had to ride to the rescue, three times on the trot, to fill up the blue minibus, more dereliction of his official duties when he should be concentrating on getting the portable appliance testers to stick (more chance of locating the governors' mugs in a coffee drought) to their schedule. The testers, we are informed, will not be rummaging in cupboards or drawers for the portable appliances, dashing hopes of a full recovery for the complete coffee set.

A thorough investigation of who set off the malicious fire alarm, eight minutes after close of the school day (a real time measurement, not taking into account those circulating twenty-four hours in advance, from the previous day, on a floating crutch), has been undertaken. The matter is so serious that the culprit, when found, will face immediate and permanent suspension, the guillotine being too good for them.

Various lines of inquiry have been initiated with the headmaster's burning question, 'Who was out of the lesson at the time, due to a call of nature?' taking precedence. (Might as well kill two birds with one stone to see who is flooding the toilets as they set light to the place.)

Leaving no stone unturned, the headmaster, heroic in his duties, revealed that he would be going 'above and beyond' by inspecting the 'call of nature' log (rather him than me). However, the results have proved inconclusive. The late timing of the incident (a criminal waste of a good drill) meant that all the pupils, even the stragglers, had left the building, except for those detained for prior misdemeanours. When the detention board is located, the detainees will be removed from the list of suspects.

Ergo, everyone has been asked to keep their ear to the ground for vital information that could lead to a potential arrest (except for a pupil reportedly wearing a Batman earring who must be apprehended if seen – unclear, yet, as to whether we are apprehending the pupil or Batman), but, so far, no names have been put in the frame.

Shockingly, even as I write (I can never get the last word with either mother, class, or own child), there have been further updates on the fire alarm incident that will leave you stunned. Or you would have been stunned, had you been standing in the way. It turns out that the fire alarm was not caused by a reprehensible pupil, but by a chair swept off its feet. No mention was made of how the chair got carried away, or from what height (a little nudge in the right direction perhaps), but placing the blame on a spurious chair, banging its head against the wall, in a suicidal moment akin to stray bunches of keys launching themselves at the guillotine, sounds suspiciously to me like not wanting to stump up for the 'false fire alarm' engine call out fee. Bearing in mind the punishment for the crime, 'suspension', there is the possibility that the chair could topple and break the glass again if Big Mac doesn't do the job securely, and I know that a poor workman always blames his tools, but Big Mac really is up the creek without a pair of small, yellow fibreglass steps with blue top holster.

In other news, the student teacher coordinator is offering a free lunch to any two members of school staff prepared to have lunch with a group of delegates coming into school for the 'school experience day'. This opportunity is open to school staff only, or no doubt Stuart would be taking up the luncheon offer. I suspect that only one spare volunteer will need to be found as Bob Bailey, head of PE, a man who not only savours his lunch but has perfected the art of charming the dinner ladies so that they heap praise and extra helpings on him in equal measure, will be game. Being head of a department where timescales don't matter and there are changing rooms that double up as holding pens, away from the public glare, means that the PE department has a more relaxed Mediterranean attitude to the lunch hour.

A truer reflection of the school experience day, away from the anomaly that is PE, would be a lunch-free day with only limited access to any other facilities on offer, although the general lack of daily hydration usually helps with the latter.

The 'lure the unsuspecting' day needs to take a tour of one of the English rooms, where an exercise book has been reportedly jammed in the printer (possible photocopying rage – the big photocopier is out of action again), holes have been poked into the teacher's desk (no weapon details divulged yet) and the projector has overheated.

As far as the excitable projector is concerned, I'm not one for putting two and two together but there have been a lot of e-mails recently stressing the need to check the guidance ratings on DVDs, especially if you are planning on taking children on a long coach trip. Apparently, all the DVDs the children bring into school must be checked for the guidance rating as, in an 'eleven to sixteen school,' some of the children are under the age of eighteen, although there are some oversized brutes in Year 11 that, quite frankly, I have my suspicions about.

Of course, the projector may simply be too hot to handle because someone neglectfully left it on overnight, but no one can lay the blame for that at my door. I cannot even turn a remote control on, let alone off – not because the technology is ahead of me, but because some thieving little fingers have gone for the battery collection. There is more chance of negotiating the release of a chair suspended by the Chippendales from Big Mac than getting him to part with new batteries; he's not big on fripperies. However, as I don't like the projector bulb shining in my face in the first place (too reminiscent of 'we have ways and means of making you talk,' although that could just be the modern foreign language department's teaching style) I'm not unduly worried.

'Eloise of Lourdes', the veritable angel of mercy, continues to thrive in the ice making business, ice being the panacea to every bump, lump, and thumping. She has also reported increased sales in sick bags and buckets. I'd like to see her myself, over migraine headaches brought on by an intense beam of light shining directly in the face, but the queue, from those stepping out of their parent's car, directly into the angel's office for the immediate stamp of approval for return to sender, is too long. Those not granted approval to turn tail upon arrival continue to pester relentlessly throughout the day to see their saviour, and sometimes, when you don't have the luxury of twenty minutes to yourself in a lesson (ten minutes to get changed at the start and ten minutes to change back at the end) you get worn down by the repeated requests for those wishing to go on a pilgrimage. I don't know what she's putting in the sips of water given to those feeling sorry for themselves, but the pupils are queuing up for it and I think you should get your name down for some.

PE teacher, Racing Billy, the fervent studier of runners and riders, is the latest to boast a strange request. Throwing his own hat into the ring as to 'who can be the strangest', probably contravenes the rules of gentlemanly behaviour for the betting syndicates he runs.

Racing Billy wants to know if anyone happens to have any experience of Clay Pigeon Shooting. He has a GCSE PE student who is using clay pigeon shooting as part of the practical assessment and he needs guidance on assessing him. Probably needs to know in advance what odds to give for the likelihood of a direct hit. Bob Bailey must be in seventh heaven with this latest practical inclusion to the PE curriculum. Once he and Billy have managed to shoot the bugger, they can charm the dinner ladies to pluck it and stuff it for the extended lunch hour. That should help to take their minds off worrying about a boy who has made a complaint about another throwing a ball in PE. The complaint has not been upheld on the grounds that 'dodge ball' is self explanatory. Not everyone has the luxury of hiding behind pupils with 'PE kit in the washer' syndrome, to help bolster their defence when stood in the direct firing line.

My son might be nearer the mark than first thought, with his staunchly held view that there is more danger from a coconut landing on the noggin than there is from smoking cannabis. The design and technology technician, Mr Tuplin, has lent weight to this theory with the startling revelation that he has fourteen coconuts. An unusual number, I know, but hardly need for the e-mail boast. His prize possessions, from the tropical, balmy paradise of the Aire Valley (white sands, azure seas, apartments in former woollen mills – eat your heart out, Judith Chalmers), are leftovers from the Aire Valley Lion's coconut shy. If you fancy one of old Tupper's 'come and get me' prizes, he will be displaying them at lunchtime, on a first come, first served basis. Now, that is what I call a birthday treat!

I'm mystified that the powers that be didn't think to put a coconut on the chopping block for the fire alarm incident; let's face it, a stray coconut has more likelihood of success than a toppling chair, any day of the week. Even better, there is always the off course suicidal clay pigeon with a penchant for the sound of breaking glass, or the practical PE student in need of refining their shooting technique to fall back upon if the fire service are a little dubious as to the chair theory. After all, you cannot blame the fire service for being suspicious when the school has more arses than chairs. The fire station officer simply can't get his head around the situation.

Stuart could do to get his head around the successful rules of holiday packing, to lessen the trauma of the three-week period prior to departure. Having detailed lists, checked in triplicate, six times over, to cover every eventuality from the weather to the medical to keeping hydrated (the pot boiler most useful) is not purely for my benefit. The way that Stuart carries on, anyone would think that I'd fourteen coconuts smuggled into my case; it's not as if I deliberately look for excess ballast. However, I trust three weeks of the heated car seat will have him nicely acclimatised for the layering up process needed to reduce the fine on the return leg journey!

You will find out how we fare, along with the number of times I purportedly put Stuart's back out (it's painful to listen to) approximately one month after our return. This is because you have made it (I can hold my own when the situation warrants it), on to the exclusive postcard mailing list, a treat for the recipient, if not the sender. Anyone would think I was mailing (I have the ear) with the Penny Black, not airmail, now that postal costs, in addition to the postcards, have been factored into the holiday expenditure.

Yours truly,

Beth

PS If any guests call in on your birthday make sure you 'let them eat cake', not the Florentines, raising a glass of the finest coconut milk!

In a Tight Corner

02.07.17

Dear Cassie,

Meg was not remotely interested in my generous offer to her of our suitcase weighing device, with slightly overstretched but still working spring, for her forthcoming trip to Rome. She is confident, apparently, in being able to pack a suitcase that doesn't breach weight limits and order a cappuccino, fluently, in Italian. The pot boiler similarly spurned.

Stuart does not share this confidence and continues to worry as much about luggage weight limits and paying for 'froth', as he does his other hobbyhorse, the weight bearing capacity of the loft. (The loft weighs very heavily on his shoulders and it is an area I have to tread lightly.) Well, when the case handle shears straight off in her hand, she'll know about it, as Stuart can testify (although you would think thirty intervening years would have been long enough for him to get over it), but it's no-good coming crying to me after the event.

I have warned Meg that it is always a trickier balancing act on the inward bound flight than the outward bound, but she replied as she doesn't collect cobbles, or go in for the home-made cosh, it won't be an issue.

One tiny, little pebble can hardly be described as a cobble, in the small mementos stakes, even if it did end up with a 'fifty-pound excess' price tag. The whole sorry experience, from some years ago, and Stuart's wrath, has quite put me off French rock sample collecting. If only I'd remembered the precious stone, a gem at the price, tucked discreetly in a sock, it could have been jettisoned before we reached the check-in desk, but hindsight is a wonderful thing. It's a sobering thought to think what the French will extort for Brexit fees, when they can hold a grain of sand for a King's ransom.

Meg does not believe in bringing home any little gifts, gratis or otherwise from her travels – apparently the notion is as outdated as anaglypta; not everyone appreciates a quality wall lining with durability as well as a surface you can repeatedly wipe clean. However, she is a massive fan of her parents returning with gifts in abundance, especially if they have the Abercrombie and Fitch tag.

Now, it is no easy task shopping in America for this brand when Stuart and I are not adapted for night vision. On our recent American holiday (glad you enjoyed the series of postcards by the way, good to know that someone can see the funny side of a situation), we had been in one store for over two hours, cloyed with some sort of fine mist suspended in the air, aggravating the airways, trying in vain to root out something in Meg's size to not bring home disappointment. We are not so long in the tooth that we don't know that the brand is for figures aimed on the small size but there is small and there is ridiculous.

In despair and with an increasing risk of developing tinnitus, Stuart insisted I fetch an assistant to help us in our quest. The girl was very polite and could clearly recognise the agitated signs of a less than enthusiastic, overheated shopper about to throw himself headfirst into a cool box. (Have you seen the size of the average American cool box? I would suggest the over eager border guard giving the order 'spring the trunk' change tack to 'spring the lid' to look for his missing hombres.)

'How old is your daughter,' the assistant asked helpfully, 'because age is what we go on to help with the sizing?' – which I find a little discriminatory for those on the wrong side of fifty. Do you know how embarrassing it is to say 'twenties' when it turns out you have found your way into the child store, completely oblivious to the knowledge that Abercrombie and Fitch have separate children and adult stores? It is nearly as embarrassing as asking three big beefy policemen in Washington, 'Do you know where we could get a coffee please?' It's not nice being asked, at a time of heightened security, if you are a couple of jokers in a less than friendly way just because you don't recognise the Starbucks logo of the building that the three are leaning up against. Anybody's eyes would be smarting after the Abercrombie and Stitch Up experience – they really are very pricey – and as far as Washington's finest are concerned, it's not as if we're not trying our very best to get up to date with the latest handheld fashion accessory to help blend in with the crowd.

Learning from our experience, if ever you have the misfortune to be in a store that relies upon shopping by touch alone, the tip is to have a bright beam and a pair of earmuffs handy. I have tried things on, Cassie, in the name of motherly duties, that have not only made Stuart blanch but left me needing cortisone injections, due to injuries sustained in trying to get back out of them, and I don't even get so much as a stick of rock, or indeed any form of rock, for my sterling efforts. Well, that's offspring gratitude for you.

On the school front I am getting quite behind with the latest developments, but I will try to go through them in chronological order.

Design and Technology are really fuming, not over the fire-retardant rating of all the illicit foam dumped in their doorway from 'Alice', but because the brand new, state of the art, rotary trimmer that the department ordered five months ago is still missing. It was dispatched on 31st January, although if the department really want to pique interest in the dispatch date, 'it was dispatched six days after Burns Night' might be a more useful way of getting the information disseminated to the wider public. There is conclusive proof that the item has been delivered to school, and to some extent the thief with the ethical conscience must be admired, because the empty box has been found in the cardboard recycling room, regrettably not with the brand-new rotary trimmer inside.

Design and Technology want to count their chickens that they've got paper to trim, when it has been shaved to the bone in every other school subject. The art department may have the green light to set a child in Plaster of Paris, for the purposes of modelling, to provide an extra writing medium, but it is not a luxury afforded to all. Envy aside, the prized trimmer, which is extremely expensive and vital to GCSE courses, must be returned immediately. Failing that, if anyone would like to send an anonymous note as to its whereabouts, the design and technology department is prepared to collect. The small guillotine will not be used as a punishment for the crime as the perpetrator leads the way in the cutting-edge of technology.

Following on from 'Alice', the drama department's next performance is 'Shakespeare Unplugged'. This production will take place in the main school hall. The event is being promoted as a mash up of food, music and Shakespearean performance. Following Props Honeypot's request for a full-length mirror (the vanity of the man) and 'bulls eyes' for the Shakespearian production, the food will have to be a mash up, or how else will anyone be able to get down the taste of authentic Elizabethan England?

The food technology department and members of Year 10 have been tasked with the food preparation needed to produce two hundred portions of the eye watering dishes, and I can only hope that the mashing technique has improved since my last stint in food technology. I didn't think I could go too far wrong with the instruction, 'Place the boiled potatoes into the colander to drain and mash', until little squiggles of mashed potato started to squirm, like writhing maggots (usually observed in the biology choice chamber when investigating invertebrate taxis, and harder to round up and count in than condoms), through the holes of the colander. 'Not the sense they were born with' as my late Nan used to say, never more apt.

Racing Billy has made his contribution to the production with the gruesome discovery that a car, parked in the visitor bay, a silver Honda Civic, has the vestiges of a bird protruding from its front grille.

You must admire how the healthy grilling method is really getting through. Honeypots must hardly be able to contain himself at the thought of a whole suit of plumage, rather than his usual request for individual feathers (fine feathers make fine birds), although the alteration of the lines to 'Eye of newt and toe of frog, Wool of bat and tongue of dog, Adder's fork and blind worm's sting, Lizard's leg and Civic Honda's wing' at this late stage must be causing some trepidation for a flawless performance.

To add to the sense of pox and pestilence of the times for the production (we now have four confirmed cases of chicken pox), the English department has requested pupils not to forget their Hamlet mousetraps, as if the proliferation of lice legging it up lanyards isn't enough to contend with.

The one-man band that makes up the head and body of the sociology department, Simon, is holding a sociology surgery – not before time, as supply teaching in that subject has always left me wounded. (Leaving woolly instructions for the class to 'doodle their thoughts and ideas' for the lesson is akin to handing the supply teacher a knife to cut their own throat.)

Anyway, Simon has put out a reminder to say that he will

be available, every Thursday, at twelve forty-five to improve technique. I'm assuming about sociology, but you never know. I could improve his technique with two little words, the two most important words in supply teaching, 'Copy Out'.

The school nurse (Child and Family Nurse, RGN, RSCPHN, Queen's nurse – more letters after the name than can fit on a pint pot), has also been offering advice about careful positioning techniques and is far less reticent than Simon. Apparently, to achieve true satisfaction you must have your front end perfectly aligned with your rear end, stray birds permitting. As someone who is in and out a lot, she wants people to think of the lamppost and line up accordingly, when positioning, so that she can achieve re-entry seamlessly. And if you can't park straight can you at least have the decency to turn the dripping hot water tap off properly in the ladies' toilets because this is a further frustration that she has all the time in the day to sit down and fret about.

The one school group that won't be worrying about a dripping tap are the school caretakers, who on their usual work scale of 'can't do, to not a snowball's chance in hell' will no doubt be clean out of washers, but at least this approach offers a shred of comfort and hope for the dehydrated, withered and wilting school governors.

The projector in the school main hall has been replaced by a more powerful unit. Unfortunately, the lectern cannot control this (ideas above its station) new projector. Ill discipline through the restorative behavioural approach is clearly spreading. I suppose a restorative chat will need to be set up between the lectern and the projector, according to the restorative justice guidelines that we are supposed to be following (a straightforward telling off no longer in fashion), and if the projector still won't play ball (along with the multitude of warring factions in the school playground – 'he's gone off with my ball' etcetera, etcetera, oh the tedium of it), escalation to a restorative conference will be called for. Failing that, the school receptionist has a remote control for the projector in the reception office but has made clear that when the remote control follows in the footsteps of the small, yellow fibreglass steps she will not be responsible for looking for it. She is inundated, trying to track down the confiscated mobile phone record sheets that have gone missing from the general office, in addition to the previously mentioned detention sheets.

Word of the Week – Confine: verb, to restrain or imprison. An apt choice of word considering the situation the school child finds itself in; there is nothing like rubbing salt into the wound.

Thought of the Week – 'You can't put a limit on anything. The more you dream the farther you get.' Michael Phelps.

Don't worry, Michael, the portable appliances and documentary sheets of evidence have well and truly got the message.

Yours truly,

Beth

PS If suitcases had had wheels thirty years ago, the loss of the handle would not have traumatised Stuart so. It is not easy to move a large, heavy suitcase, lacking wheels and a handle, with no trolley available, and wiser not to laugh when the bearer deems the situation a 'no laughing matter!'.

PPS When are you going to pack a suitcase of your own?

No Bed of Roses

28.08.17

Dear Cassie,

Following the successful day trip to London earlier in the year, after my long refusal to visit, Stuart is now pressing home his luck with tentative hints about revisiting Scotland, last endured on honeymoon, thirty-two years ago. Neither the passage of time nor the benefits of the high fibre breakfast can erase that memory. Anyone misguided enough to think that Scotland is a good choice of holiday destination, when no serious, self-respecting postcard collector is interested in images of stags, sporrans, shortbread, or the stinging rain, is going to be sadly disappointed.

To stave off and deflect the Scottish problem I am coming up with holiday destinations of my own choosing. I don't think that Stuart has anything against the Midlands per se, other than the exceedingly irritating accent, but he does visibly quail at the suggestion of Stoke on Trent or Wolverhampton.

Stoke on Trent is the home of Moorcroft Pottery, and as I am in the Moorcroft Collectors Club, it is only fitting that I should be allowed to visit periodically. Wolverhampton is the home of David Austen Roses and although I am not in the David Austen Club I should be as I have approximately ninety (thirty if Stuart asks) of his roses. I tend to plant three together and say it is one beautiful bush, so he is none the wiser.

Being a member of the Moorcroft Collectors Club did not exactly help our cause when Stuart and I got lost in Los Angeles several years ago. Through no fault of our own, due to an earlier traffic incident closing the road, and leaving us trapped in a traffic jam for four hours, we were directed off the main seven-lane highway as we journeyed a mere twenty miles, from Los Angeles to Pasadena, to see the world-renowned Huntingdon Rose Gardens. (Stuart was amenable to this garden visit as customs regulations on the transportation of live plants meant that he would not have a thorn in his side for the return leg.)

Four hours' preparation time is clearly inadequate for those tasked with finding the yellow diversion signs to help the wary and weary traveller on their way. When you need to keep your eyes tight shut for most of the journey – seven lanes are very hairy – some sort of assistance wouldn't go amiss. It's a miracle I saw the McDonald's sign at all, although I could actually recognise it without the need for police assistance (memories of Starbucks in Washington), when under such severe navigational distress. However, see it I did and so off we veered for much needed sustenance. Those looking for any opportunity to chill, by turning the air conditioning up to maximum and the heated car seats' setting down to minimum said, 'Off you go and get the coffees, I'll stay in the car.' Smart move when you are sending others into the lion's den.

When every man, woman, and child – well those tall enough to see over the pancake stacks in front of them – turn to stare at you as you walk in, you get an inkling that it isn't going to be a Betty's of Harrogate experience (although even Betty's gold-plated cream tea manages to bring Stuart out in a cold sweat).

A bright pink little holiday skirt and snazzy white cotton top somewhat clashed against the ubiquitous black vest and hanging low, practically defying gravity, baggy jeans look. Not all ethnic groups go for the Fitch cling. Maybe if I had fully embraced body art the contrast would not have been so stark, but the Moorcroft Club only share a monthly brochure and there isn't a feature on body art design when their primary focus is floral vases.

As an art teacher, Cassie, with a specialist area of interest, you might have had the confidence to say to the nearest virile male, 'Can I examine you from head to foot to give you an assessment level?' but I was in the market for a coffee not a suitor.

Having chosen to wear the wrong thing was the least of my worries. A flamenco dress with a haughty, imperious clack of the castanets would not have helped with the order. Seemingly, we had strayed into the offlimits Hispanic district.

I was so nervous by the time it was my turn at the counter, I had thought of making a run for it, but a desperate thirst and courage shown in the face of teaching Year 11 maths over the years willed me on, that my order came out as 'Twoez, coffez, por favor' (I'm nothing if not well mannered).

I deliberately omitted muffins from the order in case the Spanish translation, 'Twoez muffinez por favor' was as difficult to fathom as bun is to those from the Home Counties.

However, the modern foreign language department would have been proud of my efforts because the girl behind the counter unexpectedly lapsed into English and said 'Geez, I love your accent', which has given me faith in my Spanish pronunciation and a realisation that I must be getting more out of the Spanish lessons than I had previously realised. 'Ole!'

This is more than can be said for the enrichment lessons (a life shortening experience for those unfortunate enough to have to teach said lessons) which, mercifully in September, will be coming to an end. Instead of one afternoon per week being devoted to the enriching experience, activities that do not fit the regular timetable, the fun, frolics, and fervent messing about will take place over one whole day per term. The extended convivial party atmosphere is to be rebranded the ACE day, A Chaotic Experience, and hydration is downtown Compton, with or without gang tats, holds more appeal.

The enrichment (endurance) lessons for ICT – information, communication technology – have centred mainly on pupils producing a board game, a last-ditch compensatory effort to appease the subject's guilty conscience as it is the rise of ICT that has sounded the death knell for the board game.

I have never enjoyed playing board games in the first place (too many vexing memories of 'play nicely with your brother') and I like making them even less. A more realistic task would be how to scavenge and plead for material suitable for making into a board within the school setting. Sugar paper simply does not offer the rigidity that the standard board requires, no matter how many folds are made, despite origami now featuring in the enrichment programme.

The art department generously donated one A4 sheet of card – it's good to know who your friends are in times of need: the resource department demanded payment up front before any card could be released, and the cardboard boxes in recycling, that could have been cut up, scissors God willing, had been removed for evidence following the missing rotary trimmer debacle. Taking coffee with Latino gangs is one thing, but turning one piece of card into five loaves and two fishes is entirely another. And I am simply not prepared to line the pockets of the resource department any further when it has had more than its fair share of enriching from the scrap value of keys and an actual 'matching' – yes that is what I said – 'matching' pair of gloves.

Admittedly, I could have seen a man about some decent quality upholstery foam, but how many sturdy boards have you seen made from foam? That said, being able to cut letters of the alphabet out of the foam, to produce counters for the new school game 'alphabet report' might be a sharp move.

Some pupils, those highly pissed off with school life – I empathise – are being given 'P' reports and the two 'P's we are looking for are politeness and positivity. Others are being put on a 'S' for 'support' report – don't think it's linked to stockings or uniform, so your guess is as good as mine on that one. And all pupils have been put on a pathway – when I find out to where I will let you know. Pathway, without a shadow of a doubt, is going to overtake 'reflection' in the meaningless word stakes. If all pupils were encouraged to sit down, be quiet and listen, we would all be on the same path and wouldn't have to reflect on those that have veered off and bunked off, heading for an early fish lunch (the lucky devils), without so much as a roll of the dice.

I am, however, thinking of creating a board game of my own – how to get the adult child to move out of the home in one to three easy moves, one gaining the star prize. During a recent trip to North Norfolk (Norfolk, the Lake District, the Yorkshire Dales and North Yorkshire Moors all approved holiday destinations – Cornwall miles off the list), when our defences were down, no chance to pull up the drawbridge, our son returned home, lock, stock, and barrel plus George Foreman Grill. It has been a horrible shock, both the unexpected return and the state of George.

This is what happens when people choose not to use their degree for its intended route and follow the path to the pub. Ending up a chef, to avoid living at home after university (hostelry accommodation proving somewhat more alluring) has finally, after several years, not panned out. But my voice is as unheard at home as it is in the RPSE Christmas lesson as I shout, ever loudly, 'no room at the inn'.

We are all trying to adapt to the situation, but it is far from easy. If boots, baton, and a pair of handcuffs suddenly appear on the doorstep, to go alongside the rest of the gubbins, it will be Stuart and I moving out. It's not as if we have anything left in to eat because George Foreman has gone through the freezer with an insatiable appetite, and needs to learn that chicken breasts, salmon fillets and sirloin steaks are distinctly not for weeknights.

Yours truly

Beth

PS Never heard of Judith Chalmers? Stay behind, I will speak to you later.

Putting on a Show

21.09.17

Dear Cassie,

Do you think that Racing Billy and Bob Bailey would be happy to introduce mole killing to the GCSE practical element of PE if I suggested it to them? It would seem to me to be a more useful option than clay pigeon shooting and is a transferrable skill that I wish Stuart had been taught when he was at school. I'd have more use of it right now than all the 'sex education' and 'how to spice up your evening meal' lessons put together.

Professionals – I have had to call a proper bona fide mole man in to do the job correctly – don't wear gauntlets on the proviso that you might get your fingers chopped off when setting the spring, or on the notion that moles dislike human scent. Who cares whether a mole prefers Jo Malone or Daisy; the point is the blighters need to be eradicated from tunnelling the lawn into a sponge.

As for the gluttonous creatures licking their lips at the thought of the impending autumn bulb collection, I am a woman on a mission. I'm ahead of the game by purchasing, in bulk, red hot chilli powder which will be spread liberally and frequently over every pot of bulbs planted. Mouse, shrew, squirrel, vole, no need to distinguish; all will have their tongues on fire, begging for mercy, before the day is done. There is nothing more disheartening, other than enrichment lessons, than animals thinking they can sit down for the gratis gourmet dinner service.

For the resolute rabbit – they really do take grazing to a whole new level – Stuart has resorted to borrowing his friend's air rifle, but a clay pigeon would make more of a dash for it than a rum rabbit having its dinner under fire. And take it from me: the wearing of Lincoln green doesn't do anything to hit the mark.

To compound matters further, the lodger has spotted the arsenal of weapons we are using. How much umbrage can someone take from the fact that they weren't allowed an air rifle as a teenager, or that the Animals of Farthing Wood are enjoying a spicier meal than he's ever had? My son ought to consider himself exceedingly fortunate that during his upbringing yoghurt wasn't considered dicey and to be treated with caution (too many fermenting bacteria requiring a dash of Domestos). Had it not been for the fact that the local dairy produced exceptionally good Jersey Cream, and had a reputable brass band, I'd still be waiting for the yoghurt moment now. In much the same vein as when the lodger left school and got his first summer job at the dairy.

As an important member of the 'cheese and curds' department, with own blue hair net (you have to be on the safe side when you are the owner of easily traceable, naturally curly red hair – I have never got over the shock but do appreciate the true meaning of 'a shock of hair'), he was allowed to bring home free yoghurt. However, the freebie excitement, Stuart in seventh heaven, was short-lived. The yoghurts were the flavour of fresh air, albeit tangy Yorkshire air, because the Dairy Queen could not 'be arsed' to deliver, a persistent state that has reigned over many things for many years.

If the lodger could be 'bothered' to get himself a girlfriend, my mother could complete her CV, which began passed the eleven plus aged nine, two years earlier than any contemporaries – and don't we all know it seventy-one years on – and end with a bountiful number of great-grandchildren. I'm not sure what I'm supposed to do about the impasse; I'm already supplying the cot. I like to keep things until needed and resent the term hoarder. The lodger should be grateful (baby matinee sets included) that he can identify, recognise, and name the foods, undisguised with spice, put in front of him.

Have you decided how you are going to enrich your own life, Cassie? I have it on good authority that there is more choice out there than the bay leaf, although I would err on the side of caution with Chinese Five Spice, very overrated. Forget the art department's enrichment option of knocking up a model with the use of a cardboard box, gaffer tape and gypsum. (What an unholy mess, by the way, Modroc for crafting makes, more footprint evidence than fingerprints. Why, when we had an accidental water spillage one child went home modelling concrete boots.) Give serious consideration, as I have mentioned before, Cassie, to some of the things you could do now that you are not shackled by the school day. If you are struggling to think of what to do, I have no shortage of suggestions.

Flower shows rank amongst my favourite days out, although I must say, it came as something of a shock (not as much as the red head at birth) to see armed police at the Harrogate Autumn Flower Show on Saturday. It was quite unnerving and not at all what you expect to see amongst the prize chrysanthemums.

When I observed the heavily armed police presence, I sent the PC a message straight away to give her the heads up to get her name down for duty at Tatton Park Flower show next year as, a) we would be able to see her, and b) she would have plenty of time on her hands to pick up some urgently needed horticultural tips. (You would think a window box wouldn't be beyond the realms of all possibility.) Well, we soon got short shrift when we said the officers at Harrogate could now tackle the thorny problem of roses (or moreover, if they had been listening to the talk by the Rose Society, instead of constantly circling the burger van they would), but Stuart said we should just be grateful that they are taking flower security seriously.   Joining the RHS, the Royal Horticultural Society, would get you access to Tatton Show on members day, when all the general riff raff is kept at bay. It is more exciting than a visit to Stoke on Trent and Wolverhampton in one day. This is because Moorcroft Potteries and David Austen Roses each have a stand in the main arena and as I frequently point out to Stuart, who can be quite tense at these affairs, members get a large discount.

Last year we had the added excitement of seeing Monty (not the general but of Gardener's World fame), but television can be deceptive because you didn't have to stand on tip toes to see him. I've seen taller weeds, or should I say in next door's garden at least – obviously not my own. I'm fastidious on that score.

The National Trust is another option you may wish to explore, although I must say that the lodger and the PC were never very enthusiastic visitors, practically bordering on the downright sullen and rude. If a place of interest didn't involve wearing a wrist band and having the body spun, flipped, twisted and propelled against g-force they often didn't want to know. They still hold some seething resentment that Jekyll as in Gertrude, one of my favourite garden designers, turned out not to be the partner to Hyde, but had they embraced the membership more keenly they would have had a finer understanding of these points and be able to distinguish Lutchyens from a loofah.

Alternatively, if you favour castles over stately homes then English Heritage may be a better option for you, but you need to remember that a mounded embankment is not up to much in terms of garden design, too much trampling underfoot when the marauders invade. These are just ideas, not orders (it is not nice to be considered dictatorial) to help you get started off. But before you sign up to a whole new world of exciting possibilities, it is important that you are brought up to date with the latest school happenings.

The modern foreign language department (you can really feel the sense of desperation) is now trying Russian taster lessons. The Chicken Chow Mein mustn't be going down too well if the department has had to resort to Borscht for bribery. No need for e-mail interception, the Ruskies probably got wind of the food technology department's boiled cabbage soup wafting somewhere south of the Urals.

The Waterside bus service will be leaving Waterside at 8.02 am, which is three minutes earlier than its normal departure time. For those who struggle with both the learning of Russian and Chinese, further clarification has been given with, 'this will obviously result in the bus arriving three minutes earlier at each stop'. Clearly not that obvious. The maths department will be under further strain because children do not like studying transport timetables at the best of times, let alone bleary eyed. Mrs Drinkwater, press ganger of the supply teacher, who put out the message, ended with 'thanks Mrs Drinkwater'. There is nothing like a little bit of self gratitude for getting your name into print.

Any potential new school librarians need to get ready to put down an important date in their diary. That's a department that knows how to live life on the cusp. Instead of being given the date to write down there and then, they need to excitingly prepare for its forthcoming release. No wonder they are in the reminders business.

Another school group living life on a knife edge is Year 11. A high and potentially dangerous platform, that pupils have been warned about in advance, is in place for the final year group photograph. The guillotine is still missing, so perhaps knocking a few from a great height is the next best option. Further warnings of 'be fully dressed and please don't forget to smile' (the planning has been nothing less than meticulous) is not that easy for those teetering on the brink, nervously loosening (against orders) their collars, awaiting an uncertain fate.

For issues relating to the 'student voice', the School Council has let it be known that anyone wishing to get in touch with 'suggestions or concerns' may speak to a member of the School Council. A dignified use of the voice, if I may say, and an infinite improvement on the customary screaming, screeching, and shouting that prevails at every lunch and break time.

The 'Alice in Wonderland' school production DVDs are now ready for Blu-ray. As far as the Blu-ray is concerned, I cannot see beyond Jacques Cousteau (a cousin of Judith Chalmers before you ask) and the wonders of the ocean deep. And it doesn't stop there, I know that I have brought the blue model penis to your attention – thanks in full, three times over should go to me on the bulletin notice board for having to handle that one – but there is now the blue tooth emerging to go alongside it (breastfeeding mothers beware).

Stuart said that it was extremely embarrassing when we recently visited a car showroom to look for a replacement car and I showed no interest, whatsoever, in the salesman's fevered pitch on bluetooth speakers. Apparently, asking pertinent questions such as is there adequate space in the front passenger seat to accommodate the picnic basket with large flask, or is the dashboard on a slope because we don't want any more accidents and spillages, is not compatible with those interested in bluetooth speakers, now that making your own coffee, in favour of a handheld Starbucks, has gone out of fashion. If the salesman had mentioned a heated car seat, he might have sparked a bit of interest, rather than promoting sound when a driver and their passengers should be concentrating and driving in silence. I have strong views on the need for silence in a car, much the same as my philosophy for similar sound levels in the classroom.

The art department ought to get to grips with the revolution in all things blue and modernise its own curriculum. Georgia O'Keefe could supply an image of something very blue on the interactive board for analysis and interpretation to help capture the pupils' imagination (if the projector bulb doesn't blow), although it's not the type of flower you would see wantonly flaunting itself at Tatton Show, certainly not on members' day, at any rate.

Yours truly,

Beth

PS The pupil misspelling of the week, 'b day', was not text speak for blowing out the candles. Try harder.

A Trifling Affair

10.10.17

Dear Cassie,

We have just returned from a delightful trip to Madrid and Toledo. You would have been impressed to see me trailing after Stuart to one art museum after another (he's very keen on art), including the Prado, feigning interest, when I'd much prefer to be sitting in the botanical gardens than pretending to understand the warped mind of Salvador Dali.

I said to Stuart, 'Any painting with the name The Great M–' (I can't actually bring myself to say such an appalling name – if you're in the dark, ask the PSE department – it's more their line of work) – 'isn't going to be suitable viewing, and certainly not for anyone of your age.' After viewing the obscenity, I take back what I said about piquing pupils' interest in art by studying Georgia O'Keefe et al; stick to Constable – at least the British know how to do decorum and a decent tree.

Surprisingly, after being marched (Stuart has a nonflexible pre planned holiday itinerary headed 'make every second count') to see one El Greco after another, thankfully housed under one roof in the El Greco Museum in Toledo – unlike the works of Caravaggio, inconsiderately spread under various iconic Madrid roofs – I did find an artist's work that moved me. Indeed, I was transfixed when we visited the Sorolla Museum in Madrid and as a result I have found my favourite artist.

Joaquin Sorolla's work, displayed in his own beautiful villa, bequeathed to the nation by his widow, was truly captivating and the experience has made me realise that, despite your specialism, I simply do not know who your favourite artist is. Could you therefore put me straight on the matter? To make a good impression, Cassie, you may choose from Renoir, Degas (do not allow bias due to a love of ballet), Monet or Sorolla with top marks awarded for a critical understanding of the question and the enlightened answer, Sorolla!

During the Madrid visit, following my lack of Spanish communication in the Latino McDonald's, LA, I decided to keep my ear close to the ground to improve my language skills, so that ordering a coffee would be less daunting in future. In doing so, I managed to garner quite an impressive array of Spanish words and phrases for use on future holidays.

After listening to the in-flight safety instructions, I am now able to shout 'brace, brace' in Spanish, should the plane suddenly nosedive. Of course, if I were to give the instruction in English, a simple 'brace' would suffice; the Continentals really are overly excitable.

In the hotel lift I learnt the phrase 'No entrar en caso incendio'. The Americans ought to take up this phrase and adapt it to 'No entrar en caso 'Fatty' Arbuckle', because quite frankly, 'Six persons maximum' is meaningless, if each one person is equivalent to three, and six of them with luggage decide to ram themselves into the lift you are sharing. 'Brace, brace, brace, brace, brace,' in a frantic high-pitched wail doesn't begin to cover it.

'Silencio' is another addition to my burgeoning vocabulary, and next time the headteacher is showing visitors, or prospective parents, around the school I shall prepare the class with 'Silencio, brace, brace' and hopefully any visiting entourages will walk right on by.

On the home front, the lodger has got a part-time job as a delivery driver for the local bakery whilst supposedly studying some IT courses (present rate of tuna fish consumption, odds on for the dorsal fin before the IT certificate). It is a wholly Italian-run business – only the lodger could manage to seek out the Mafiosi – but as with the local dairy experience, the taste of a strawberry cream tart has been made up entirely of freshly whipped air.

The WPC commented that the delivery driver isn't at liberty to start handing out free cream horns whenever he pleases, even though his mother does have strong cravings, and it was completely the right course of action to take. There is nothing as sanctimonious and righteous as those in authority with a few police powers going to their head. I retorted, 'He is not driving a gold bullion van, we are talking éclairs here,' but apparently that is the thin end of the wedge. Well, a thin end would be preferable to no end at all.

I am not the only one with strong cravings (in my case unsatisfied) as the science department has recently found to its cost. The hunt is on for a black cherry jelly thief, a scoundrel, who utilised a golden opportunity (packing up) in the dying seconds of the science lesson prior to lunch to bag the loot. The gelatinous product had been placed on the teacher's bench, by the science technician, in readiness for an experiment to be carried out after lunch. But the product was swiped from under the very nose.

The science department, justifiably scandalised – the taking of scientific materials is potentially dangerous – has put out an all-points alert to apprehend any pupil found in possession of black cherry jelly. The department does have an inkling who the culprit may be but at this stage of the investigation is not prepared to share sensitive information with the wider teaching staff. The science department, having donned its thinking cap, is working on the theory that black cherry jelly could have been taken for the purposes of consumption.

Well, you can see from the gravity of the situation that this is no trifling matter. As a dutiful citizen I casually asked the Baker's Boy if he had noticed an upsurge in jelly-based products in the back of his van, but he was very tight lipped on the subject, saying it was an 'ask no questions type of workplace'. Then I checked with those 'in the know' about dangerous materials and asked where black cherry jelly (yet unmodified or adapted – I'm picking up all the relevant spiel, and I feel ready to personally sit the exams on the police rule book) ranked in the offensive weapons act? The response was withering and given in the tone usually reserved for 'I don't need a man or a garden in my life, how many more times?'… Clearly not enough times – it is all very well being able to drive on a motorway unaided, now with the blues and twos flashing, but just wait until there is a mouse in the pantry and then she will know the true value of a man.

I have been marooned upstairs all day since Stuart left for work this morning saying, with parting shot, that a mouse had shredded his luxury Dorset Cereal box (how do the so-and-sos know to go for the most expensive cereal, cocking a snook at the Weetabix) and gnawed through the red plastic lid of the Bourneville cocoa powder tub. There is nothing like going on a hunting raid of someone else's property and then having the audacity to sit back and relax with a mug of cocoa at the end of an evening's work. I wonder if the rogue jelly thief is feeling quite as relaxed, with the temerity to call in at the hub (previously known as a sin bin but now a social centre with computer gaming for the misbehaving) to see if the restorative justice practitioners manning it could supply the custard with impunity. I will save my thoughts to you on the value of restorative justice in the education system to a later date.

Now then, returning to the science department and the wobble it finds itself in. Without the benefit of police assistance, I do not think that the department has been found wanting in its own perceptive surmising of the situation, with the enlightened idea that the jelly could have been taken for consumption, especially with the offence occurring around lunch time. My only criticism would be that rather than letting us check every pupil for sticky fingers, deep cherry lips and a black tongue, the department goes for the direct approach of pouncing on the 'inkling' to save everyone's time and trouble. We can only hope and fervently pray that the inkling is a birthday partying mouse and not a giant rat.

Royal jelly, as opposed to the disappearing cherry type, is on the agenda for the Bee Team, a group of like-minded enthusiasts who think they are the bees' knees as they wax lyrical about honey production. Incentive to join this group include the opportunity to dress up (personally I would call that type of dressing up a fetish, not haute couture) and the chance to handle a hitherto unknown dangerous substance, with potential edible opportunities. I think I'll stick to collecting postcards, thank you very much; I'm not cut out for extreme sports and hobbies, although if you are really pushed for ideas, you could always give it a go.

Well, I will end with this week's words and thoughts for your deliberation and delectation.

Word of the Week – Illusion: noun, false appearance, or belief. Very apt when it comes to creating a stiff, sturdy board out of sugar paper.

Thought of the Week – 'Books are uniquely portable magic,' Stephen King.

Not quite as magic, Stephen, although decidedly portable, as a roving pair of small, yellow fibreglass steps, chairs that spontaneously set off fire alarms and vanishing black cherry jelly. Portable magic comes in many guises and I am sure that if Mr King would like to pay the school a visit, he would have extensive research for his next horror tale without even having to touch on matters pertaining to behaviour.

Yours truly,

Beth

PS Not to be outdone by Tupper's old coconuts, Big Mac will be proudly displaying his babies at lunchtime. Apparently, they are on the small side but very fresh. So fresh, in fact, that he only unearthed them at seven o'clock this morning. If you have a yen for the freshly dug potato, kindly let me know.

Counting the Losses

05.11.17

Dear Cassie,

Strange request man, Racing Billy, really does want to win the competition for being the strangest; his sporting gene for winning at all costs just keeps on bobbing to the surface. His latest desire is for 'face paint'. Anything that does the trick, Billy lad. He's hoping that staff may have some 'kicking about' at home (it's a very limited vocabulary), in grey, brown, and green colours. Sadly, he's not signing up for the Territorials but needs the slap for his boys' performance in the gym and dance show.

Now, I like camouflage as much as the next person, particularly when I choose my outfit to blend in with the colour of the nearest sugar paper backed wall display, but performers, even dancing boys, would surely be better to be seen on stage than hidden from public view? Although I must say, as parents, we never encouraged our son to be into that kind of thing.

Talking of the interloper (preferred title – heir to the throne), just to give you the heads up, he's discovered that I am writing to you, and apparently, if he is made the subject of any correspondence, or if his name is mentioned in any way, shape or form, with typical filial gratitude, he will sue.

I digress, back to Racing Billy and his plea for free cosmetics. I think this latest ploy is a cunning plan to stock up on clay pigeon shooting necessities; obviously Bob Bailey and he have been too visible, and the clay pigeons have got wise to their moves (all forms of dance considered) and as a result, the 'Billy Bobs' are now trying the stealthier, undercover approach.

The intrepid hunter-gatherer duo are not the only ones empty-handed. The school governors – you must feel for them, you really must – are not only without coffee mugs but now their drinking glasses have gone absent without leave, compounding their dehydrated state. 'Eloise of Lourdes' 'miracles not happening this week' note on the matter was rather curt in tone: 'If you have removed twelve glasses from room G4 return them immediately.' There was no 'please' involved or an offer to collect without punishment or sanction.

It's not as if the governors could be offered a cool 'tinnie' to quench their thirst because the ladies in the school office are frigid. No, that can't be right, slip of the tongue, what I mean to say is, the ladies in the school office are without a fridge and are desperate for a replacement. 'Has anyone got a spare or unloved fridge that they are getting rid of or thinking of updating to a newer model? If so would it be possible for the office to take ownership of it? Ours is on the way out.'

There was no mention of how the present fridge was

leaving the confines of the school office – theft by the clean getaway burglars (the last school break-in was through the storeroom housing all the cleaners' cleaning materials), an act of defiance against being owned and seen merely as an object, or simply following in the footsteps of the small, yellow fibreglass step ladders.

Putting the governors on a drip is probably not in the school nurse's (admirer of the alphabet) duty book although I am sure she could be relied upon to provide the latest, up to date, educational thinking on what to fiddle with in a crisis. Fidget toys. It is a blessing, therefore, that 'Eloise of Lourdes' can be relied upon to supply the ice cubes needed for cracked lips, to help take the governors' minds off the lack of suitable reading material available to them, especially since the latest book losses.

The English Department, no marks for originality, has come up with the same old story: 'A box of books has gone missing'. Targeting and capturing the audience is as fundamental to all English lessons as the evaluation is to RPSE, but having such draconian teaching methods can hinder creativity. 'We have checked all of the English rooms which make us 'suspect' (that's called tension building and possibly worthy of a half mark on a good day), the book box has travelled further afield. (Further afield, as far as I can see there is an audacious convoy on the move.) Can you check all rooms for a large dark green box containing 26 copies of 'An Inspector Calls'?' Although when he does, he will have to knock because the emergency hand bell, for use when the automated electric bell develops laryngitis, the teacher's curse, has followed the crowd.

Locate the convoy and Mrs Drinkwater might be able to retrieve her missing banner. The banner, used at parents' evening and other events in school, has disappeared from the small store cupboard located outside the special needs office. Extraordinary. Not only are objects leaving school en masse, under their own steam, but they are waving a banner to triumphantly champion their deeds.

In other matters, away from school items on the run, including the block of thirty scissors reported missing by the geography department (could be anywhere in school but any set looking out of place must be handed over immediately –it's not finders keepers), the music department wish us to know that the Boom Whacker club will be on Thursday, not Tuesday of this week. Any club known as the Boom Whacker Club would do better, in my opinion, to not meet on any day of the week. Have these people not the slightest idea of the excitement generated by an overdose of onomatopoeia? I belong to the 'el silencio es oro' club. (Hand me a star for the wall chart.)

The resource ladies, sounding like a broken record, have reported that the photocopier is out of action again. 'The engineer has been summoned, please bear with us. Audible groans all round.' Make of that what you will but there is hardly the need to broadcast such matters. This is the trouble with social media and up to date communications, more information than is necessary, giving a blow-by-blow account of everyone's deeds throughout the day.

Not to be outdone by the needs of the resource ladies,

Minibus Marlene has called a man in of her own, brazenly hiring a seventeen-seater, including the driver. I didn't realise the school was so flush. Tabletop sales of foam products must be on the rise, although you won't catch me purchasing the pupil homemade sponge, unless I have witnessed, first-hand, the stringent hand washing process.

On the home front, a family party was held to celebrate my parents' diamond wedding anniversary. My mother's quiz on the year 1957 was not easy to answer, as other than my parents, no bugger at the party had been alive in 1957. However, I have gleaned some facts for you that may just come in useful the next time you are involved with the trivia of 1957. Nellie the Elephant was at the top of the charts. We know this because we had to endure the full parental rendition, accompanied with Nellie the Elephant actions (don't ask), aimed at recreating walking along Blackpool seafront at the time of the honeymoon.

For the obligatory quiz, family members were divided into teams of two, and when asked to name the Prime Minister of the day, the PC and her cousin relied upon listening in to other teams whispering the answers to each other, (a form of cheating) and came up with Matt Millan. I hope when Meg's taking statements, she will pay more attention to the accurate naming of suspects and not rely on hearsay. Shame on the PC as she studied history at 'A' level. Mind you, she did a geography degree but does not know where any country in the world is, but evidently, as she frequently points out to me, that isn't what geography is about these days. Clearly not, if the geography department can't name the location, and give a six-figure grid reference for pinpointing scissors left in uncharted territory. (I have much cause for despair.)

I was teamed up with my sister-in-law (of birthday the day after Burns Night fame) but it didn't help when it came to 1957 because it appears that she is more au fait with post millennial than pre-millennial and she thought it was more my era of expertise. She will be lucky to get a birthday card three hundred and sixty-five days late next year.

I thought I did rather well to come up with the answer 'a pressure cooker' for the question 'what was invented in 1957?'. If I had heard the question correctly, through all the raucous noise and arguing (you don't need to join the Boom Whacker club with a family like mine), I wouldn't have given my sister such gleeful satisfaction (she's very competitive and likes to think academically superior – ' I would just like to say at the end of the day which one of us is the headteacher with time management skills and the ability to pack for a family of four in under thirty minutes, without contravening weight limits') at the thought of a pressure cooker and not Sputnik, the correct answer, being launched into space.

I went for the pressure cooker because it was the only concession to modern day technology that ever graced the home as a child, and despite the condescension generated by my answer, until my mother got the hang of the pressure cooker, quite frankly, with the head of steam it built up, it could quite easily have launched itself into space. So, I wasn't too far off the mark.

If the pressure cooker had relied upon battery power it would never have seen the light of day, and to this moment in time, I can't shake the battery guilt complex instilled in me as a child. The calculator – to my mind, the greatest technological revolution of the nineteen seventies – was not only abhorred for the cost of its batteries but for playing its part in the decline of mental acuity. Ask the head of PE, Bob Bailey. My mother taught him at primary school and he once confided in me that he still suffers from post-traumatic stress syndrome induced by the daily mental arithmetic test that was used to kickstart the day. No wonder he had to learn to thwack a straight rounder to impress.

After the Diamond Wedding celebrations, at October half term, Stuart and I went to the Lake District for a four-day drenching. It would be lovely to report a ten-minute break in the deluge, but it was conclusively wall to wall wet.

We always stay at the same pub because it is cheap, cheerful and provides a hearty breakfast. However, on this occasion, when we went down to breakfast, the chef was wringing his hands. Due to stock control mismanagement, instead of the full English, he could only offer the 'lite' bite. Talk about it never rains but it pours. Well, my disappointment knew no bounds – I am not a lite bite sort of person, and especially not when gearing up for fell walking. I said to Stu, I can't walk on an empty stomach; we need to change plans and hit the garden centre instead.

The next day we got the 'full bite' twice over. Stuart remarked if I hadn't glared so much the previous day and made tutting noises, the chef wouldn't have given us yesterday's missing breakfast with today's all in one go. I said I can't be responsible for a chef's guilty conscience and it's not my fault that we've been stuffed to the gunnels so that we are incapable of standing up, let alone fell walking, with yet another garden centre day in prospect. I mean, is it too much to just want a happy medium in life?

Regardless of the breakfast shenanigans, and going away to try our best to escape, the mobile phone meant that we were still on hand to dispense advice to our hapless offspring. 'When sorrows come, they come not single spies but in battalions.'

The PC rang to say she had broken down in the car wash and it had taken four men to push her out of the rollers. I nearly needed four men to help pick Stuart off the floor at the thought of her paying for a car wash, or it could have been the after-effects of the double 'Full'.

Stuart is out of the same mould as my mother when it comes to incurring unnecessary costs. I said, 'Meg,' (reportedly in a school ma'am voice that neither offspring nor husband appreciate) 'I have never known you to wash and have a car valet before, what has got into you?' and was shocked (although clearly not as much as the car in the middle of a heart attack) to hear the reply 'wet dog'. Well, she knows my feelings on all things four-legged and the necessity to keep them out of house and auto. I mean to say, eau de chien is hardly going to further her cause, but evidently she and her friend had done the Three Peaks Challenge during Storm Brian and were responsible, after dripping all over the car afterwards, for the untoward doggy smell. Stu commented that it didn't matter if she had given a lift to a hitch-hiking storm-damaged skunk, the moral of the story was always a bucket and sponge. Upon getting the car repair bill, for what the PC could only mournfully describe as the most expensive car wash in history, we trust she has learnt the error of her ways.

The lodger (who shall remain nameless for legal reasons) rang to say that the pantry mouse had invited its friends and family to the party, and the merry band had nibbled his sack of protein powder. The lodger was not happy with my response to the news of this latest infestation and said that he was not taking the blame for being the Pied Piper of Hamelin, the timing was purely coincidental and there was no need to take my breakfast distress out on him. Believe you me: distress doesn't come close to it when you have an army of mice taking up body building.

Back to school, in real time, a mugshot of what a governor's mug looks like has been posted on the e-mailing system by Minibus Marlene. This is so the younger members of the teaching staff, whose calculator-dependent brains have not had the benefit of development through training with the mathematical logarithmic book, can recognise a mug. You would be surprised to learn that the word 'GUV,' is not emblazoned on the side, but instead the name of the school. If you possess one of these exceedingly rare and valuable items in your store cupboard, and feel that it is the genuine article, could you please hand it in pronto before its mugshot joins Crimewatch and the appeal for the 'Most Wanted'.

Yours truly

Beth

PS The tablecloth is a good place to start for the novice embroiderer. You are more than welcome to borrow my beautiful and plentiful skeins of silks. It is a fortunate six-year-old indeed that receives a lifetime's box of embroidery silks in a legacy.

Hot under the Collar

29.11.17

Dear Cassie,

The mystery of the missing mugs is small change compared to 'guillotinegate'. The large and small guillotine are now both missing with a manhunt on to find them. There has been a spate of e-mails requesting their immediate return, all to no avail, and the ladies in resources are in pieces, although clearly not by guillotining.

The history department has kindly donated a broken baby guillotine (it really does delight in the ghoulish) on the off-chance it can be repaired. I suppose calling in a guillotine engineer for the resource ladies will make a change from the services of the photocopying engineer, and they do say that a change is a good as a rest.

The situation has become so critical that subliminal messages have been placed in the pupil daily bulletin, in the form of the word and thought of the week.

Word of the Week – 'Investigate': verb – to search or inquire into with care and accuracy.

Thought of the Week – 'there's a way to do it better – find it' – Thomas Edison.

Heads will roll on this one, Cassie, mark my words, although Racing Billy won't be rubbing the back of his neck in trepidation. He is far too busy putting out requests for newspapers, especially the sports sections (special area of interest horse racing), for his GCSE PE class. It is a wonder he hasn't highlighted page three for his boys to settle down and relax to after a spot of clay pigeon shooting.

A further investigation has been launched by the resource ladies into 'hot drink drinkers'. More costly Public Inquiries in the offing. Some unscrupulous members of staff, too idle to walk down six flights of stairs in a five-minute opening, have being tipping the remains of their coffee beakers out of the tower block windows. The resource ladies, with considerable skill and aptitude, have managed to catch the liquid coffee, before it hits the ground, on their open windows below, and have the streaks to prove it.

Thank goodness the resource girls have managed to hold onto the possession of something tangible at last. The governors can breathe a sigh of relief that they are off the hook for this one. Let's face it, they haven't got a pot to piss in (the budgets are very tight) let alone a mug to brew up in. However, the incident does help explain the rationale behind the head of Year 11's latest recruitment drive, a man looking for any staff members willing to take on a potential mentee, to help mentor them through the treacherous waters of Year 11. Bloody treacherous waters, one could say, if the mentees are going to be swimming through hot coffee raining down from on high, en route to the examination room. However, the bar has been set remarkably high in terms of the criteria needed to become a mentor of a mentee, felling the candidate list in one fell swoop. So, don't go sharpening your pencil for the CV, just yet, because 'you need to be human'. Shucks, that's torn it!

The geography department, in addition to rummaging in cupboards for the missing guillotines, has been scavenging in other ways, with a 'Scavenger Hunt of the Atlas'. Who in their right mind would set the question 'What is the capital of Ukraine?' when the answer only leads to excessive excitement on the merits of last night's tea, or 'dinner' should one be a headteacher or school governor.

When studying the causes of flooding, we had the benefit of nature in action, with yet another lesson ending in tears. The lesson followed the lunch hour, formerly called dinner time, and so I was taken aback when a girl asked if she could eat her lunch in the lesson.

Quite reasonably, in my opinion, I said 'no', because the lunch hour is the considered time for luncheon and the classroom, not the dining room, is only for those reliving the delights of last night's Chicken Kiev. However, the 'request denied' approach prompted a deluge of tears from the girl and a tidal wave of class antipathy towards me. It's hardly my fault if there has been some sort of incident (the details were very sketchy), at lunchtime, involving two unnamed but clearly unsavoury and unpalatable girls (rapprochement not on the cards), bringing on a momentary loss of appetite.

Feeling under more pressure than when trying on Abercrombie and Fitch on the behalf of others, I had to reluctantly give in to the girl's request, to stem the flood and rectify the perceived injustice the masses were campaigning about.

Providing a maître d' service ('would you like any sauces, mustards or condiments, madam?') I moved the girl to a table at the front of the classroom, where she would have a little more privacy, yet twenty-five minutes into the lesson and the girl hadn't got to her crusts. There is nothing like a leisurely lunch when there is classwork to be done, even if such careful mastication prevents my performance of the Heimlich Manoeuvre. God forbid anyone would wish to rush on my account.

The girl should have been naming a large country beginning with T, bordering both the Black Sea and Mediterranean Sea, not sit savouring it at a leisurely pace, between two slices of a little seaside town beginning with R, found bordering the Sussex/ Kent border.

Once the flood situation was under control, I had to move on to geography's other hot topic, the climate, or more specifically the classroom microclimate. There is just no pleasing some. Keeping the windows shut is for the benefit of the pupil, not to the detriment. The head of geography might be able to get children to sit still with a stiff upper lip – he knows how to make a man of them (don't you wish we had all had the benefit of military training) – but in my lessons the off-course wasp or bee can generate more hysteria and mass panic than a girl with one sandwich short of a picnic.

One very persistent boy repeatedly and dramatically requested to see 'Eloise of Lourdes' – he was hot, he had a headache, he had a heat rash, he could hyperventilate (St

John's Ambulance must have been visiting again), he could faint (he was beginning to sound like Stuart on a road trip), he simply had to loosen his collar, on and on it went, until it came to the end of the lesson when he donned hat, scarf, coat and gloves to move on to the next indoor lesson, ambient temperature Baltic.

Rather than drawing attention to the dietary requirements of different countries in the scavenger hunt quiz, or stressing about the naming of hot, dry landscapes, a more pertinent question to ask would be where is El Dorado located? Considering the excessive number of glue sticks, colouring pencils, pencils, pencil sharpeners, paper clips, paper reams, plastic wallets, felt pens, rubbers, rulers, drawing pins, blu tack, sellotape and staplers with actual staples (impressive) – alas no scissors, but then again, nobody's perfect – the answer would appear to be the geography classroom. The department has got more resources than chocolate chips diving headfirst into the healthy muffin.

Members of the geography department are not the old fossils they claim. (Share and share alike not widely practised.) Indeed, the geographers positively rock when it comes to providing the tolerable enrichment lesson. All points of the compass leading to the 'remain in your seats, no talking' film option – North by Northwest, The Golden Compass, East of Eden – (would madam prefer popcorn or a Magnum?). And I would tentatively suggest a sweep of the storeroom could potentially unearth five craft knives, three adhesive spray cans, one large and one small guillotine, an expensive – I'll just emphasise that again, very, very expensive – rotary trimmer along with a decent quality broom. The recycling of the rotary trimmer cardboard box is the icing on the cake. The geography department is obsessed with sustainability, religiously rewinding, and replaying all film tapes.

The pious RPSE department has also been religiously recycling, considering the process, virtuously, from a moral and ethical standpoint. Unlike the geography department, its conscience is clear.

The new style end of term enrichment programme, the ACE Day, is looming large and this has prompted the RPSE department to get in on the recycling act with requests for old wallpaper rolls that may be 'lurking about' in people's cupboards. The skulking rolls are needed to allow the pupils to sketch on the back of, although no judgements will be made on patterns. I should think not. RPSE is a holier-than-thou subject when all is said and done, although the removal of the evaluation must be causing shivers.

Word of the Week – Lurking: adjective – remaining hidden so as to wait in ambush.

Thought of the Week – English department – up your game before the RPSE department steals a march on tension building.

No mention was made of anaglypta rolls. I have boxes of them in the loft (part of what some family members term the hoard – hardly the Lewis Chessmen). I prefer useful items that will become required the minute they are thrown out and careful patching is required. On this basis, I am toying with the idea of throwing out my beautiful Silver Cross pram, and cot with sumptuous, broderie anglaise deluxe quilt and bumper set, in a bid to prompt a grandchild, but can't quite control my heart rate or agitation when it comes to putting this notion into action.

As it is coming up to Christmas, Stuart will have to make a foray into the loft to extricate the Christmas tree and the treasures that bejewel it. A tense operation requiring careful handling (apparently, I own more baubles than branches), and placation and mollification of a husband that likes to make a song and dance of the task.

'More baubles than branches' is a better situation to be in than some siblings I could mention who are 'all tree and no baubles'. Well, apart from a smattering of handmade child decorations, looking dated (there's a skill to hoarding), with facial features designed to attract friends of the pumpkin. Seemingly, it is terribly infra dig to have a beautifully coordinated, and exquisitely adorned, silver and pale turquoise (no bawdy reds or flashy golds) bauble-laden Christmas tree when the spartan shabby chic approach is the way to accessorise amongst the higher school rankings.

Having an extensive greetings card collection in the loft, all major celebrations included, with complete sets begun by my mother from my first birthday onwards, and now proof of the changing nature and style of greetings card over the last half century, does not lighten Stuart's mood. As an artist, Cassie, I think you would be interested to see how styles have varied with the passage of time, and not take the Philistine approach of some that I could mention. The lodger and PC have about as much interest in their own collections, begun and saved for from birth, literally (sadly I'm lacking my own welcome to the world cards), as the class tasked with studying Fleming's left-hand rule of electromagnetic induction. It is on a par with their interest in the Silver Cross pram and cot with sumptuous broderie anglaise bumper set, and so I don't see why I should shoulder all the blame, when other family members won't take responsibility for loft space clearance and help an irate husband reach his model railway.

We will be spending Christmas Day with my sister (all tree and no baubles) and the rest of the family in North Yorkshire.

The lodger and PC are great admirers of their auntie, anything from the minimalist look to the succulence of the turkey (am I the only person on the planet giving serious consideration to salmonella?), to the house mutt named Macduff (pseudonym for the mutt with a confidentiality paws). Actually, it is a pedigree with its own hired personal trainer (dog walker) – for the professional who knows how to delegate time management and has appeared on the Yorkshire Vet (the dog not the trainer).

My children also admire my sister's contemporary colour schemes, no rhyme or reason. I expect pigeon with smoked trout trim to be on the Christmas dinner menu, not on the walls – no wonder the dog is looking peaky. Sorry, my mistake, the colour is called Pale Hound, not peaky looking dog, in case you are tempted to do a spot of Farrow and Ball redecorating over the festive season!

Yours truly,

Beth

PS In case you are of the same school of thought as the PC

– that geography these days is not about knowing where anywhere is (I blame your shared interest in Love Island for the little grey cells deterioration) – the answer to the quiz is Turkey on Rye.

PPS I have all the cards you have ever sent me, treasured, catalogued, and stored in my collection.

Highlighting the Problem

15.12.17

Dear Cassie,

The politically incorrect school housekeeper, hot mug Mrs Braithwaite, responsible for washing the school's dirty linen, but not her own mouth, was in full flow upon hearing the latest problem to hit the playground as described, in gory detail, by the deputy headmaster. 'I don't know what's he's worrying about,' expounded Mrs Braithwaite, 'the little bastards only shit everywhere when all is said and done.' Well, my ears pricked up at that, I can tell you, behaviour must be really going down the pan if the so-and-sos are resorting to those sorts of dirty tactics. After all, this is a school and not the back of the police van.

However, it turns out that Mrs Braithwaite was referring to the less than pleasant habits of the school yard seagull, not the disgruntled school pupil protesting its innocence.

It has come to light that the pupils have been stamping, with intent, on highlighter pens at breaktime and lunchtime, in a bid to extract the inside of the highlighter pen. Once freed, the inner is placed into a water bottle to create 'coloured water' and the 'coloured water' subsequently sprayed and squirted around the playground. Now, as a mother, my first thought would always be for the white school shirt, not the action plan and seagull healthy eating lesson plan (hard to believe we don't have one in play), but I suppose the deputy head needs to get his ducks in a row in the event of a claim. Forewarned is forearmed. Apparently, the seagulls (no sense of direction) on the school yard can choke to death on the debris left behind from the stomping game. Consequently, we have been asked to stamp down, heavily, on any pupil witnessed engaging in such a nefarious activity.

Obviously, Mrs Braithwaite, incontrovertible seagull slayer, is no friend of the off course 'shitter', her words not mine!!

Personally, I blame the art department – there is far too much emphasis on 'go away and experiment with colour,' and now the pupils are taking your advice seriously. Mind you, it is better advice than that dispensed by the PSE department for sex education purposes of 'go away and experiment with a mirror'. (Something to do with being familiar and comfortable with body parts in the privacy of your own bedroom.) Goodness only knows how the department evaluate that homework task, something along the lines of 'have you got one below, at, or exceeding all expectations' I shouldn't wonder. Both 'experimental' departments should follow the supply teacher's advice of do not deliberately paint the face, shirt, work, or table belonging to your nearest neighbour, wilfully knock over the water pot, or spend too long preening in front of a mirror.

The design and technology department has lost its colour and sparkle (positively wan) following the theft of a hefty consignment of glitter. I assume it is a hefty consignment, being of a certain age – one that appears to put me in the same category as every pupil's grandma, without the actual grandchild – means that I have no conception of how much space 500g of gold glitter (ordered from YPO but not delivered) takes up.

So far this week, the litany of grandma comments have included, 'Your glasses chain (not always a guarantee of finding them, even when slung round the neck, but less burdensome than the entire school community having to do a sweep) is like my grandma's', 'My grandma always uses that word' – the word in question being 'the pictures' instead of the present-day fetish for the cinema – and 'My grandma feels the cold as well, Miss'.

You don't have to be a grandma to feel the cold in the history block; it is a refrigeration unit, not a trio of classrooms. No one need look towards me for the missing glitter when I have my own covering of frost. However, I know that glitter is your sort of thing, Cassie, so you need to keep your eye out, or possibly shut, should any knock-off come your way, approximately one lorry load's worth. The silver, red, green and baby blue glitter pots are also untraceable, along with a specialist side order of Pixie Dust in 'Tickled Pink' (somebody will be). Traumatised and out of pocket, the design and technology department has made an emergency appeal for donations. As always, the department is willing to collect.

How optimistic is it, that Racing Billy, man of many needs, will return the goods during peak glitter season with a boys' gym and dance show no doubt on the horizon?

In other miscellaneous school news, three boys are not in school uniform and are wearing PE shorts due to an incident on their way to school with a can of expanding foam. The mind boggles. As if the 'little shitters' haven't enough to contend with in their day. The boys' mothers (sinking under the weight of the washing) have been informed. Why is it always the mothers that must shoulder the responsibility for teenage boys? I'm sure the fathers would have far more idea on the uses of expanding foam and know how to spray responsibly when in the vicinity of pen-eating seagulls.

The ladies in resources, in addition to losing two guillotines, two boxes of headsets, the chargers for the school cameras and a laptop, have now lost the very air that they breathe. It is almost like a game of 'my mother went to market' (a game that my mother always had to win, by the way, with no allowances made for age, as she didn't believe in allowing children to win – character building tactics), rebranded as Racing Billy Raided Resources and retained...

Anyway, I digress, the lack of air is not, as you may be forgiven for first thinking, Cassie, due to the tight shutting of windows to prevent the tossing and sloshing of drinks from towering heights, or from the pebble dashing of windows in a multicoloured hue, but due to the invasion of personal space.

The head's personal assistant has written a hefty tome on the etiquette of photocopying. It is an incredibly detailed and exact rule book, but the following excerpt should give you the nub of the rules.

'The photocopier at the rear of Sandra and Susan's desk

is for the sole use of Sandra and Susan and no one else. Photocopying has a forty-eight hour turnaround, not twenty-four hours, so please be patient and organised. Advanced planning is key. If possible, leave your copying in the tray on the counter, or alternatively use the staff copier, unless of course you have asked Sandra/Susan's permission to breach the barrier, in which case please be mindful of Sandra/Susan's personal space.'

God forbid anyone should breach the barrier and breathe the rarefied air of a child-free zone or knock into the engineer shackled to the machine. The girls want to think themselves exceedingly lucky that they are not sharing space, as I must, with the 'little bs' (Mrs Braithwaite's influence again), and I don't mean the seagulls.

Yesterday I spent a listless day in ICT, looking at the advantages and disadvantages of playing computer games, an exercise only marginally ahead of a game of hunt the mirror. When I told the class that I had never played a computer game in my life, it prompted one young man to say, 'It must be very boring for you with nothing to do.' Obviously that young man has never reached the dizzying heights of loft clearance duties on a Saturday afternoon to concentrate the mind.

When I commented further that I did not use a mobile phone, another pupil was extremely concerned for my very survival, asking what I would do in an emergency. Storing multiple packs of toilet rolls, bought in bulk from the cash and carry, in the loft, is part and parcel of my survival planning, despite the lodger's unnerving point that when the food runs out, the toilet rolls will be false economy. However, thinking positively (the school rule), I still think my advanced planning will be of more benefit than the survival text sent to the pupil 'find a doc'.

In addition to toilet rolls, seemingly of ever diminishing length (no puppy claims these days for tripping up, under no win no fee), I have five, extra large, 'one hundred and twenty wash' boxes of washing powder because I will, if nothing else, be clean, and at Stuart's last count, two years' worth of dishwasher tablets blocking access to the festive features.

I have not had to endure the annual tirade about my 'loft collections' this year because a certain person is not in my good books. The person in question has been caught, red-handed, watering down the Flash bathroom spray, as if a professional cleaner of my standing wouldn't notice a spray with no cleaning power whatsoever, in a bid to save money because I am, apparently, too profligate with it. I hold no truck with this sort of penny-pinching behaviour, and I am using this transgression to my full advantage until we can extricate the tree.

The pestilence problems continue unabated with a flood thrown in for good measure. When the settee was repositioned, in preparation for the Christmas tree, the carpet underneath it was found to be sodden but with no obvious reason for it being so. The plumber was duly summoned (it's catching) and he found gnaw marks that had pierced through a plastic connector, on a water pipe under the floorboards which had caused water to spray upwards. Not only have the mice had the audacity to feast on Dorset cereal, swilled down with a mug of dreamy cocoa, they have created their own spa to go alongside the muscle building gym. It is beyond belief; I said to Stu, if the traps aren't working, we need to be more creative and try the highlighter pen approach.

The lodger has been highlighting, relentlessly, the benefits of digital currency technology. As I have yet to use a cash machine (I take very seriously the threat of muggings, hidden camera fraud and the possibility of the machine gobbling the money back up) I am not the best person to embrace digital currencies. However, after not being able to get my breakfast in peace for several weeks, during fervent explanations of the wonders of block chain technology, I have capitulated and made a small investment. I do not know where my money is, I do not know how to get it back out and I don't know how to use it, but hey man, I'm in the game. If only the plumber had gone digital!

Lastly, I received a beautiful Christmas card from the PC, with a verse that meant a great deal to me. I can't share the lodger's festive verse with you because no doubt it will be subject to encryption and hidden in a digital wallet. As for a man in deep disgrace, 'I promise to never dilute again' doesn't have quite the right tone to it. However, I am unashamedly going to take the words from the PC's verse to pass on to you because it captures the sentiment I wish to express to you in a nutshell: 'If snowflakes were hugs, I would send you a blizzard'. I am not normally driven to such displays of effusiveness, it is not in my nature, but as it is Christmas and considering your plight, I make the exception.

Have a wonderful Christmas tucked up with The Etiquette

of Photocopying. That is, if, as instructed, you managed to
get your name down early for a copy.

Yours truly,

Beth

Not up to Speed

06.01.18

Dear Cassie,

It goes without saying that there was only one winner of the Christmas family party quiz, the grammar school competitive streak holding out as strong as ever, with an 'unkindness' of ravens gaining the crown. If the younger generation is ever to be given a sporting chance, form period time needs to be devoted to general knowledge and learning animal groupings, not sitting around in a circle discussing pass the problem.

I am not a fan of New Year either, too much germy kissing in public places, with the added burden of having to brush up on Burns Night.

A certain disgraced member of the family household needs to brush up on speed limits. I don't need to open a penalty notice for a £100 fine plus three points (three more than they scored in the Christmas family quiz) to the driving licence, upon returning home from the final day of the autumn term, when I am already a coiled spring due to a surfeit of flashing reindeer antlers. I always knew that teenagers had horns (an ill-timed non-uniform day requiring PAT testing).

Well, my fury knew no bounds, blood pressure readings rocketing, but as I pointed out to 'pedal to the metal man', there would be no need to lose sleep over what to spend any Christmas present money on because every penny of it would be going towards Her Majesty's Constabulary Christmas Bash. I could have had one hundred bottles of undiluted Flash bathroom spray for the privilege.

Of course, the fine gave the Baker's Boy all the ammunition he needed across the Christmas dinner table ('they are very sneaky, Dad, it's not your fault') in his usual tirade against the constabulary, finishing with his well-worn line, 'to think that your daughter is one of them'. Germane, I must admit; you would think that we would be entitled to family discount but apparently not. Indeed, there was little sympathy from that quarter – 'Read the signs, Dad, it doesn't matter if there are signs for a dual carriageway, if it clearly states 30 mph at the start of the dual carriageway.'

The Baker's Boy, jubilant and excessively relieved, in my opinion, that the notice didn't have his name on top (I fear for the cream slices) says that I can't keep using the excuse of boy racers – practically pensioner racers (the man can't even get his leg into his pyjama bottoms without toppling over) – vermin infestation, the restorative approach to school discipline and an inferiority complex to my mother as the source of my high blood pressure, conveniently failing to mention his own contribution to the rising mercury. Instead, he points the finger of blame towards the humble potato (Sir Walt, what were you thinking of?) and every other food high on something called the glycaemic index.

To ward off the prospect of being publically named and shamed on the 'only a matter of time' diabetic sugar offending register (unflattering to be termed a chocolate cake dealer) I have unwittingly gained a campaign manager for 'don't stop it, swap it'. It is the New Year mantra.

To get the day started, not a bowl of chaff floating in whey, but preserve on wholemeal – note not white toast – I thought I would swap my raspberry jam for the rather tarter taste of Seville. However, before the marmalade had a chance to escape the jar, my campaign manager swooped down from upstairs, with more speed than the value of my plummeting bitcoin, to warn that I might as well use a hypodermic needle to give myself a sugar shot.

The chance would be a fine thing when I am under such strict food surveillance. It is quite a strain having to go under cover in one's own home to extract a biscuit from the hidden stores. ('If you are hiding it you need to admit you are an addict before progress can be made, Mum; have a taste of your own medicine and see how you like it.')

'The cache', according to the speed machine, is precisely why we found a mouse's nest under the display cabinet housing the stockpile, and which came to light when we had to move the cabinet, along with the settee, to make space for the joyfully released Christmas tree. Can you believe it: a selection of After Eights, Elizabeth Shaw and Bendicks mints had clandestinely joined ranks, behind my back, without the chance for the appropriate rodent risk assessment.

The PC ought to be considering the merits of the cocoa pod while there is still time. Cocoa trees, evidently, are dying out through climate change. Despite this highly distressing news, cocoa-based products did not feature on the outlandish list of food items requested, in advance, by the PC, for her Christmas homecoming. A list featuring fruit teas, couscous, red topped skimmed milk (through actual free choice, not the antics of a cream guzzling brother) and wholewheat pasta (we don't even do pasta let alone wholewheat pasta), with no requests made for steak and kidney pudding, stew and dumplings, or my mouth-watering favourite, meat and potato pie with red cabbage. It will be sun-dried tomatoes, at home on the autopsy bench not the pantry shelf, before we know it, if we don't take a stance.

I can't understand it; Meg knows that her father single-handedly does the food shopping and that he's not naturally drawn to the exotic. When first married, accusations of a cavalier attitude and an inability to spot an offer – coupon collecting not up to degree level – were more than enough reasons to make me throw in the food shopping towel, leaving my husband sole martyr to the cause.

Consequently, it was left to me to point out to the PC that her father couldn't even spell couscous, let alone know which aisle to go up to find it on. What's more, the man had enough on his plate because there had been a run on brandy cream, pigs, and sprouts. (I may not be allowed in the store, but I'm still treated to a tense, desperate, running commentary, by virtue of the mobile phone, as if I've the ability, with a click of the fingers, to summon the pigs in blankets cavalry.) Therefore, to prevent further agitation and deviation from the standard list, could she make do with a hot Ribena and a tin of semolina?

The fruit tea question (sometimes I think I was handed the wrong baby) was not the only question we had to ask the PC over the festive season.

On New Year's Eve we went to a party (mercifully lacking the educational quiz but with a bountiful, beautiful buffet) at some friends' who have a daughter the same age as the PC and the two are also good friends. I confided in the friend, who had just got engaged and bought a house with her fiancé, that we wished the PC had a man and a house in her life. Afterwards Stuart commented, 'Have you ever thought you might be on the wrong track and her friends know something we don't?'

'Like what?' I replied and was shocked, bordering on traumatised, to hear 'I think you should replace the word man with partner every time you ask her friends to set her up with a blind date'.

I said, 'Stuart,' (allegedly very sharply, but not quite as seething as the tone reserved for why on earth didn't you clock the speed gun; saying it is pitch dark at seven a.m. in the morning is no excuse?') 'a liking for fruit tea and couscous doesn't suddenly make you bat for the other side even if it is all the rage in Manchester.'

My mother would have apoplexy if she knew. She doesn't believe in the humble teabag, let alone fruit tea, when tea should be made directly with loose tea leaves.

But once the seed of doubt had been sown, I couldn't sleep and so decided to tackle the problem head on, in the manner my mother always employs: 'your father wants to know if...?'

Well, there is no need to worry: we got a very explicit answer, verging on the impolite to that one and I can categorically state that any meddling or future matchmaking on my part (although it's not looking hopeful since I have been issued with a gagging order) will definitely involve a man!

Other festive party events included having my parents for a meal, thank goodness, not literally. My mother arrived for the occasion dressed in a sweater suitable for the Hull fishing trawler, topped off with a body warmer. (If we were operating the gates of hell, rather than a thermostat turned up to 30 degrees, we wouldn't hit the ambient temperature.) My mother then presented us with her favoured bottle of red; pre opened in her own home for the aperitif at the correct room temperature, and at the end of the meal, as is her usual way, corked it back up to take home with the usual refrain, 'I know you don't like it and there's still a drop in it!'

It is coming up to the twentieth anniversary of the last time we were invited for a meal at my parents' home; however, over New Year we are invited for drinks and nibbles, with my brother (who still hasn't lost his touch for spying the biggest nibble) and his family.

As I do not drink wine (from either opened or unopened bottles), a special purchase of six Coors light beers was made for me in 2012. Thankfully, this year I have made it to the last bottle, which three years ago my mother was telling me had reached its sell-by date, though she thought it would be passable – 'waste not, want not'. For this exceptional act of kindness, I express gratitude beyond compare – after all, my parents have gone out of their way to buy something they don't use, although hardly as revolutionary as a request for couscous and red topped milk.

Despite the worries of 'is this actually safe to drink or where can I pour it out without being seen', I continue obediently to express gratitude not shown by my own offspring. 'No, hot Ribena will not suffice,' from one; 'and don't be stocking up on any of the gnat's piss that you drink,' from the other, 'it's Stella or nothing'. Yes, well, try 'nothing' now your father has been fined.

It's all very well that 'don't spare the horses' man says that he has saved the family hundreds of pounds over the years, with careful shopping and coupons, and that I should be grateful because Moorcroft vases don't grow on trees. And if it helps to make me feel any better, he feels worse than I do (although I doubt anyone could feel that cross), but it is still a bitter pill to swallow. Although not quite as bitter as toast without marmalade, oxidised red wine, an 'off' Coors Light and the mouse-mauled mint to finish off with!

Yours truly,

Beth

PS If you know what people do with pesto, answers on a postcard please.

PPS I do truly hope the start of the New Year will be everything you wish it to be.

A Close Shave

Dear Cassie,

In your continued absence the messages continue
unabated, although some of them really are nothing but a
load of old rubbish, especially when it come to the school
minibuses. Minibus Marlene knows how to hit home a point
effectively. 'Bearing in mind that no food or drink should be
consumed on the blue or maroon minibus, there is certainly
a lot of rubbish.'

Marlene's not the only one overflowing with litter. The
ladies in resources, equally terse, have requested that staff ask
for a replacement bin when they have 'stuffed' the recycling
bin to capacity.

Well, I suppose it's no good if the ladies only get to marvel
at the top of the engineer's head when a full frontal is required.

In addition to the etiquette of refuse collection, the ladies
have issued up to date guidance on the latest photocopying
law. (I'm not surprised they can't find time to press the
photocopying button, with so much effort devoted to legal
matters, guarding their own personal space – don't breach
the barrier, close all windows, and firing off electronic

communications at will as to what has been deposited on the photocopying machine (don't worry, only keys, not seagull shit in glorious technicolour), along with the implied veiled threat of don't send pupils our way to do your own dirty work. (On and on it goes – no wonder they can get a book deal out of it.)

Anyway, the latest edict is that the turnaround time for requests (photocopying presumably, not the Chippendales) has been increased from forty-eight hours to seventy-two hours and any extra finishing/ trimming may take even longer to complete, although anyone is more than welcome to complete this stage for themselves.

I assume the last part is a coded message aimed at the guillotine thief because the rest of us certainly haven't got the wherewithal for trimming – well, not since the pinking shears went west.

It is school production time again and this year the performance is 'West Side Story'. Instead of tickling those struck with stage fright with a peacock feather, Props Honeypots has requested a spare length of piping, presumably to whip them into shape. Mr Honeyman needs the underground plastic piping to make into a fire hydrant and has requested, somewhat imperialistically, that the dimensions be 'say eight to twelve inches in diameter and say two to three feet in length'. The pipe is going to be heavily modified, so if you do happen to have a spare length lying about, Cassie, it's looking like donations only.

We haven't got a functioning plastic pipe underground, since the mice sunk and gnawed their bastard teeth into it.

I still haven't recovered from the plumber, recommended by my mother, and who upon his emergency call out to purvey the sodden lounge carpet and cast his eye over the situation said, 'It's good to tell that you're your mother's daughter.'

I remarked to Stuart, 'What do you think he means by that?' I am nothing like my mother, in either looks or deeds and at least I put coffee powder into the coffee making process to avoid the boiled water experience. However, the lodger put me straight on the matter and said that it was because we both had houses, to use his words (words which my mother would say show a distinct lack of a grammar school education), 'filled with crap'. How I rue the day he didn't inherit the collecting treasures gene.

In addition to plastic piping, Props Honeypots would also like a length of chain donating. I think the resource ladies could be called upon for that one, once they decide to finally let the engineer go.

In my Christmas letter to you, Cassie, I completely forgot to ask, at the time, if you would like to be entered in the Christmas sweepstake, with a two-pound stake. Well, it's too late now because Racing Billy has already done the draw. He revealed the winner, alongside his 'famous' Simpkins homemade Christmas Cake, 'totally free of charge', on the last day of term. I don't know which is more questionable, the cake's notoriety or its cost; after all, there's no such thing as a free lunch. I suspect the sweepstake takings have helped to cover the cost of ingredients in the 'famous' cake. On what grounds the cake is 'famous', I'm struggling – a soupcon of camouflage paint (khaki), a dash of glitter (sparkly), a sprinkling of Pixie dust (tickled pink), or the clever effect of marbling the racing results, but whatever it is, he clearly thinks that the Simpkins 'blow your own trumpet brand' can give Mary Berry a run for her money.

On the home front I was right to express concern for the vanilla slices; I am quite prophetic. Apparently, it is very disconcerting to have the fruit tarts, followed closely by the chocolate bombs (confectionery not devices) and mini mille-feuilles shaving past your left ear as an idiot driver pulls out suddenly in front of you.

Fearing it could be case of 'a chip off the old block', I said to the Baker's Boy, 'Are you absolutely sure you are not to blame?' but my accusation was utterly refuted. The Vanilla Pod had to have a much-reduced order, the van required professional cleaning ('Dad, can you help me, the more I wipe the more it smears?') and I am still soaking the clothing stains.

The PC would be well advised to soak her own clothing; I suggest a daily boiling in a vat of bleach would not be amiss. It transpires that she is going into homes that don't use quite as much bathroom spray and bleach as I favour, and there is a knack to saying, no thank you I prefer to stand, or possibly stick to the floor, for those with a sole covering that little bit extra surface area.

Disconcertingly, the PC has informed us that all the years of watching the Jeremy Kyle Show (a quite unbearable programme that we have locked horns over many times due to its detrimental effect on the brain – I am more like my mother than I care to admit) is paying dividends, as many of her domestic cases are moral dilemmas, and she simply says to herself what would Jeremy advocate. I remarked, 'Surely you're not telling me that Jeremy has had an American Pit Bull in the studio?' following her latest case in which she had to make a snap 'Jeremy decision'.

The case, involving two fighting brothers, their mother, and the oversized Yank, gave me goose pimples. I was raised on the story of Albert and the Lion, my mother's party piece, full rendition without recourse to notes, and annual childhood holiday entertainment for whiling away the hours in a perpetually wet Llandudno. She's been performing on a buffet since the age of three. Well, I certainly do not want the 'PC and the Pit Bull' to become a version of Albert and the Lion, particularly with so much energy already expended on child rearing.

To cut to the chase, the police were called when the sozzled brother punched the sober brother, the mother intervened, and the US hell hound waded in for a piece of the action, or two or three, of the more spirited sibling. In the ensuing aftermath the mother, desperately taking the lead, begged for the drunken son, not sweet boy Arnie, to be put down but the pet van had already been called for and so there was no turning back. Life's a bitch!

If the cosh and cage method could be applied to the classroom, the hail-fellow-well-met salutation might be bestowed upon the supply teacher more readily. In maths this week, a Year 10 girl came into the classroom five minutes late, took one look at me and gave the greeting, 'Oh f—-ing hell, is it you?' (Only marginally less offensive than 'Oh f—-ing hell, am I having you?') Charmed to see you too, I'm sure, and so with a hello and goodbye all in the one sentence I managed to free up a spare seat in the classroom. The classes are so full that without recourse to dangling the pupils from the light fittings, there is really no means of following the disciplinary measure 'isolate the child in the classroom'. However, last week, when an odd snowflake flurried past, the pupils went into dangle mode all by themselves, freeing up the crowded seats, health and safety out of the window, and all for the chance of a lick of iced snow.

To conclude my news, Cassie, I felt my age this week (and every other week) when a Year 8 girl reported that someone had weed on the school bus going home. Is there no end to the pupils' talents? However, she looked askance when I questioned her further as to who had urinated (not the type of pupil that Marlene will want to set foot in the minibus should the situation ever arise).

'No, Miss,' cried the shocked looking girl, 'they had weed.' I sometimes feel hindered by my lack of modern-day parlance and wish at times, namely when stood in front of a GCSE maths class during a snowstorm, that I could only reciprocate the adolescent speak for good afternoon!

Yours truly,

Beth

PS Tapestry, perhaps?

A Sticky Wicket

31.01.18

Dear Cassie,

Mr Honeyman has gone into overdrive. In addition to underground piping, he now wants to know if anyone has any Coca-Cola crates to hand, failing that, milk crates, that he is prepared to paint in Coca-Cola colours.

Being brought up to abhor Coca-Cola as the Devil's poison itself, my mother was ahead of the game when it came to the suitability of children's drinks (more on cost grounds than caffeine and sugar content), and so there is no chance of finding a Coca-Cola crate in my household.

The master key for the server room and the cabinet keys for the trophy cabinet, located in reception, have gone missing from the general office. The keys were on a hook and must be returned as soon as possible, along with the missing thesauruses, in what the English department, working overtime, is calling, 'The Mysterious Case of the Missing Thesauruses'. There's a title to pique interest and one that could give 'The Etiquette of Photocopying' a run for its money. No doubt a trophy (I propose the small, yellow fibreglass steps trophy, dedicated to all things lost and found at school, although the steps themselves are still all at sea) will be awarded to anyone that can locate the case of thesauruses, once the trophy cabinet keys have turned up.

My money is on the food technology department as the culpable party because, this year, instead of making the annual plea for a pasta machine, it has upped the ante to, 'Has anyone got a dusty pasta machine in their cupboard at home that we could take possession of?'

You are not telling me the department has managed to come up with the word 'dusty' without the help of a thesaurus, although I am impressed at the fortitude required for sneaking the message past Mrs P's formidable defences.

This week's word of the week is 'Neglect' – verb: To treat carelessly, to pass by without notice, to fail to give proper care and attention to. (To lose the thesauruses irrevocably.)

Of course, the subliminal message could have been aimed at the state of the pasta machine, or more likely, the office staff, who are on the hook (shame it's not the actual keys), for failing in their duties as key keepers of the victorious trophy cabinet. It's certainly not aimed at the pupils who have perfected neglecting the school behavioural policy to a fine art and need no further clarification on the subject.

Neglect can come in many guises as the following note shows.

'Can you please inquire with the form before X's lesson as to who was sitting on the stool which X sat on so that I can pass on the dry cleaning bill for his trousers due to chewing gum?' – X is code for a redacted name by the way. I've always wanted to use the word redacted but never had much opportunity.

Now, the school may have record high numbers of teaching assistants, technicians, secretaries, administrators, caretakers, counsellors, councillors, clerical staff, receptionists, photocopiers (as in the ladies with barriers and chains, not the actual machines), plus an operations manager, librarian, data and curriculum manager, school nurse (Child and Family Specialist Nurse, RGN, RSCPHN, Queen's nurse), exams officer, bursar, accountant, personal assistant and 'Eloise of Lourdes', indeed any working group bar teachers, but what the school really needs to operate efficiently is the Chewing Detective. A true professional, not a pseudo teacher, who would really know how to get to the bottom of things.

Tracking down sticky situations, to see who has been sitting where, could have unintended benefits. Dogged pursuit of the gum trail could help to explain the disappearance and subsequent reappearance of chairs in unfamiliar classrooms. The English department, clearly not up to date with Farrow and Ball's naming colour charts and completely adrift without thesauri help, has reported two mushroom (very 1970s and even too outdated for me now that I have Elephant's Breath professionally sprayed on the walls) chairs and the grey modern foreign language department has an invasive green (Vert de Terre, surely?) plastic chair. With classes bulging at the seams, you would think that subject departments would be grateful for the humble milk crate, painted in Coca-Cola colours, not complaining about the state of the decor.

The science department has got all its chairs at home, but the pupils are still on the edge of their seats, two years after the event. Well, wouldn't you be if you knew a stool had been defiled by a poorly Year 11 boy. I don't think the science technician has ever fully recovered.

At the time of the incident, the boy's caring and considerate teenage peers came out of the lesson with the reassuring words, 'his only option is suicide'. Seeing the child and family specialist nurse (RGN, RSCPHN, Queen's nurse) for a dicky tummy wouldn't have been an option for the young man as any medical advice dispensed from that quarter is clearly reserved for the benefit of the Queen. 'Eloise of Lourdes', on the other hand – no letters to her name, but a miracle worker all the same – would have had a handy ice pack (stick it on it, up it or under it) readily available. The Eddie Waring (look him up) school of medical treatment.

Criminal damage to stools and chairs aside, the Chewing Detective wouldn't necessarily have to stick to gum (the science technician has a very good solvent to help in that respect), when sitting down to review the evidence. There are plenty of other school areas in need of a breath of fresh air.

The Chewing Detective might hopefully have some constructive ideas on how to handle misbehaviour to rival, if not better the specialist child and family nurse's (RGN, RSCPHN, Queen's nurse) advice of 'go away and play with your bendy man'. Playing with your bendy man or squeezing a blu tack ball is apparently a stress reliever for those so bored in science they have to resort to s——- (there are certain words due to a polite upbringing that I still cannot bring myself to say) their pants to get out of the lesson.

Other behavioural therapies from the child and specialist

nurse (RGN, RSCCPHN, Queen's nurse) for the child that cannot concentrate in the classroom include the doodle book – alternative title Sociology. This is in direct opposition to the supply teacher's theory of successful concentration, which is to remove the doodle book, along with the bendy man, blue tac ball, worry beads, elastic band, fidget spinner, catapult, and anything else that can be fired into space.

Self-control is a particularly important skill to master, as you soon find out when it is compulsory to learn your times tables from one to twelve by the age of six during the 'drying up' after tea, but did I wave a red tea towel and flounce off saying that I had better things to be doing when I wanted to learn capital cities, not numbers?

If children were taught to concentrate on their times tables, at both home and school, the maths department wouldn't be shown the specialist child and family nurse (RGN, RSCPHN, Queen's nurse) red card by pupils with 'I've got anger management issues' on such a regular basis, and as for food technology, the department should be grateful for help on how to wash up properly any way it can. The tea towel is as hard to distinguish from a dish cloth as a teaspoon from a tablespoon, the art of swilling off a bygone concept and the ambient water temperature of cold to tepid perfect only for congealed fat and germ multiplication. I'd like to work up a full head of steam over that one, but haven't been issued with the appropriate card.

With rampant forgery, theft, foam fly tipping, vandalism and pyromaniacal chairs on the loose, there'd barely be time for the detective to give chase to the pupil hopping home (one black Converse shoe left on the maroon minibus), or to intercept and grill (no boiling in hot oil these days) the pupils en route to 'Eloise of Lourdes'. Let alone track down a missing Super Dry black coat with turquoise zip. Super Dry, a refreshing change from the perennial piss wet shoes (pupil terminology, not mine).

The distribution, escort, and collection of visitor lanyards, with or without the threat of sterilisation (the lanyard that is, not the visitor), could be another duty, along with detailed forensic analysis of what exactly is 'Eloise of Lourdes' putting in the sips of water that has them queuing out of the door. And strong words will need to be had with the head of geography, something along the lines of, 'Hello, hello, hello, what have we here?!'

Big Mac, in need of the constabulary more than most, wishes to ascertain, with or without police assistance, who has torn the heavy blackout curtains at the side of the main hall. The cases keep on rolling in. Surely, it couldn't be one our pupils, could it (that's the danger of marking your own homework) capable of performing monkey antics, shinnying up and swinging from a curtain that can't bear the load? Although considering the chair and the fire alarm incident, there is the possibility that a pair of scissors has gone completely rogue. Support for this idea has been reinforced by the Thought for the Week – 'the true sign of intelligence is not knowledge, but imagination', Albert Einstein. How true, and I imagine being whisked away (not the men in white coats) and entering a retreat every day of the week.

Before I end, Cassie, you will be pleased to know that there is no need to go rooting about looking for old crates because Honeypots has just sent heartfelt thanks to say, 'Wow, crate crisis resolved. I am indebted.' I cannot believe I have missed out on the collecting crates bandwagon to run alongside my other more cherished collections!

Yours truly,

Beth

PS I really do 'Wish You Were Here'.

The Root of the Matter

06.02.18

Dear Cassie,

Racing Billy may have the famous Simpkins Christmas cake, but my brother-in-law, husband to the minimal mistress, and esteemed in his own field, doesn't have to rely upon candid peel to get his name into print. That said, I don't think that he has quite reached the celebrity status of his own mutt, following its previously mentioned appearance on the Yorkshire Vet.

My mother nearly fell out of bed one morning when, without prior family warning, my brother-in-law appeared on Radio Four's Today Programme, in his capacity as an electrical engineer. She was then miffed that the rest of us hadn't shared her experience.

I said, 'Mother, unless your son-in-law is going to appear on Love Island or the Jeremy Kyle Show, the PC isn't going to want to know, and the lodger doesn't appear to register anything during early daylight hours, and so even with advance warning, we would not have made a difference to the audience listening figures.' And to be fair, it's not as if we are treating one famous family celebrity more than another because we managed to miss Macduff's performance as well.

Focusing on the latest line in thefts at school, it is difficult to know whether to describe the culprit as light fingered or green fingered.

Hormone rooting powder is not what usually springs to mind to be kept under lock and key, if alas, we had the key, but this latest theft has sent serious ructions through the entire science community.

A full-scale sweep of the school had to be undertaken once it was realised that ingestion or inhalation of the powder could result in a dicky tummy and science didn't want a repeat of that performance.

Instead of following the COSHH guidelines, control of substances hazardous to health, the science department found itself under the cosh. The hormone rooting powder did not have a hazard card assigned to it, as is the case for the standard chemical, and so everyone was at a loss as to the imminent dangers the raging hormones, wandering around school, officially unaccompanied, posed.

Well, rather than donning a chemical warfare suit apt for the rogue Anthrax spore, or more pertinently, the common-or-garden germs teenagers spread liberally and profusely at will every day, the head of science took matters into her own hands and wandered up and down the school corridor, with a dustpan and brush, ready to spring into action. But regrettably, when the morning breaktime bell has signalled the starter gun for the race to the tuck shop l, no matter how eagle eyed and adept the sweeping action, there is a lot of cross contamination; although to her credit she did return with a lot of sweet wrappers.

The offending item – a round of applause please for the two lady science technicians well honed and versed in following lines of inquiry – was eventually found in the rubbish bin outside the Year 11 common room, seal intact, with the bonus that the school corridor had been given a free makeover. The thief didn't have the chance to do any snorting, ingesting or pricking out of seedlings before having to dispose of the hot flush item.

Providing free hormonal treatments (it seems to be the latest fad in the race to cross-gender), so closely on the heels of the black cherry jelly fiasco, has meant that the science department has had to review its safety procedures, and so from now on 'hormone rooting powder' will really be talcum powder in disguise. Although count me out for looking for the thief with a soft bottom in case they get itchy fingers (it could be an irritant) for a second time.

Fellow art teacher Linton has come up with a book title of his own: 'The case of the boy who asked permission to go to the toilet and suddenly and inexplicably vanished.'

E-mails abounded as to the whereabouts of the 'vanishing act', but I wasn't too concerned that the boy had disappeared down the actual bog (a graceless term, reminiscent of my own school days, when toilets were never referred to as anything other) as the facilities are permanently and deliberately stuffed with toilet paper, wilful acts of vandalism difficult to understand.

In the latest damage report to the boys' toilets, a wall mirror has been cracked, the paper towel wall dispenser dispensed from the wall, and several toilet paper snowballs successfully fired at the ceiling. However, after visiting the Tate Modern in London, and for the sake of the evaluation, I think it should be remembered that one man's idea of toilet paper snowballs as an act of vandalism could be construed as another man's idea of modern art. Even so, I trust the modern artists will quickly be brought to book.

Another pupil vanished, albeit fleetingly, when a teacher, who shall remain nameless – although I can categorically assure you it was not me – isolated them in the storeroom for misbehaviour due to a lack of isolation space in the classroom and then locked the storeroom door at the end of the lesson, inadvertently forgetting their charge was still in there. The confined, enterprising pupil risked further sanctions by ringing the school receptionist on his mobile phone, despite the mobile ban, to say he had been locked in the storeroom and needed his lunch. I can't begin to think of the ramifications of having to explain that one – there's nothing worse than the scorn of the child, three minutes late, losing its place at the front of the lunch queue.

Science is not the only subject department worrying about the use of dangerous materials and substances; art is similarly fraught.

A recent behaviour report brought to light that a pupil had taken it upon himself to paint a huge black line across another pupil's face. Whilst being reprimanded and admonished for this indiscretion, he painted his own hands, despite being told not to do so, resolutely adhering to the earlier class instruction, 'the more you practise the better you get'.

As you can imagine, this made a settled plenary and reflection impossible, although I would personally like to paint a thick black line, to the point of oblivion, through the words 'settled plenary and reflection'. From the supply teacher's perspective, I prefer: can we simply get through the lesson without magic tricks – first you see him, then you don't, gum on the bum, paint on the face, onions on the hands (or not) and jelly on the tongue; forget the learning experience and reflection, albeit with a broken wall mirror.

However, the novice student art teacher, overseeing the hand washing process, without the benefit of the paper towel, was concerned about what would happen next time, if the avant-garde artist got the opportunity to be experimental with more dangerous art room materials. Which ones? The pencils and pencil crayons are too blunt for injury (there is no shortage of pencil sharpeners, but the blades inside them have been extracted for the pupil arsenal), the PVA containers empty or stubbornly solidly hardened and the glitter pots long since fenced. That reminds me, the special needs department wishes to ascertain 'has anybody been given a packet of glittery stickers by mistake which have come from Amazon?' Very sensible, get them premade rather than the perils of being sprinkled with Pixie dust for the sake of modern-day art. And are you positive, Cassie, that you don't have the necessary equipment and wherewithal for firing toilet paper snowballs in the name of collage ceiling art?

Props Honeypots is not fraught. He is so laid back that he has put out a call for a foot pump. Not any old foot pump but one suitable for a blow-up bed that he can use in school. Can you imagine the gall of the man, everyone else is running round like scalded cocks, looking for sparkling glitter, hormone rooting powder, cherry jelly, trophy cabinet keys and a pair of small, yellow fibreglass steps with blue holster top and yet he has got the balls (still not returned to PE after the last school production) to be napping.

It must be sheer bliss, when chaos reigns, to sleep soundly during the school day without recourse to the Power Station Quarterly; I think you'll find it's an electrifying read. 'Quarterly', the Power Station Christmas Annual would be one publication too many. There's some very dry material on my brother-in-law's coffee table, nothing to fire up the imagination. However, if you are having difficulties sleeping, Cassie, I can always see if I can scrounge you a copy.

Yours truly

Beth

PS On second thoughts, Stuart's Railway Modeller Monthly, equally stultifying but three times more prolific, might be more up your street. And if you unadvisedly go for 'OO' gauge layout, instead of the 'N' gauge for 'neat', you will need the full length of the street.

In the Rough

18.02.18

Dear Cassie,

I'm pleased to report that our second trip to London, within a relatively short space of time – one year, not thirty – has been a success, although a blow-up bed would have come in handy during the performance of the Phantom of the Opera. No matter how many times Stuart poked me with a rolled-up copy of the Railway Modeller, it took a Herculean effort to stay awake. The theatre was stuffily soporific with leg room (N gauge) designed for Pod, Homily and Arrietty Clock. However, not wishing to lose star pupil status for achieving mother and husband's top goal in life – value for money – I did retain consciousness for the spectacular Mamma Mia, bellows, of either kind, not required.

In London, I discovered the delights of the Charlotte Tilbury Beauty shop. This brand name was recently brought to my attention by the bevy of girls who study the 'hair and beauty' course at school. It's amazing the information that can be extracted when a class is nailed down (not splitting hairs) for the manicure lesson that is, not the makeup thefts. I had to have my guinea pig eye out more than a Boots girl working on the cosmetics counter, with eye shadow, mascara, and eyeliner semi professionally applied.

As a result of the enlightenment and the collective advice received – 'You really need to do something, Miss' – Mateo, from Vienna, my personal makeup consultant (Stuart's comment was 'you wouldn't want a son like that would you?' – your guess is as good as mine, but my thought was, well, if he's managed to move from Vienna, at least he has managed to move away from his mamma, unlike some I know), took one look at my skin and said, 'Oh darling, you so need miracle cream, it's very dry.' And before I knew it, I had been swept along with his enthusiasm and gay abandon and paid £70 for a pot of miracle cream.

Unquestionably, I am regretting the folly of my actions, could never tell my mother in a thousand years, and can only describe the aberration as getting carried away with the heat of the theatre. It's a very desiccating atmosphere. Stuart said that the only miracle was that anyone would part with the money (we don't all need the long arm of the law in that department) and I thought that Mateo might have to reach for the smelling salts for Stu before the miracle cream for me.

I wish that I could announce the results of the miraculous unguent but unfortunately have not been able to bring myself to use it, feeling more guilt than when purchasing a double A battery and could kick myself for not sticking with the efficacious nipple cream.

Having to teach a class of Year 7 pupils how to make a pizza doesn't exactly help the complexion, especially when there is enough flour dust in the air to run the risk of the minor industrial explosion. (It's a surface area thing but I've neither the time nor the energy to go into the chemistry behind the blast.)

At truly short notice, may I say, indeed, before I even had the chance to take off my coat, I was thrown into the pizza making business as if I were straight off the Napoli boat.

The process began with the class having to make dough for the pizza base. This involved 'rubbing in' flour and butter, using the fingertips only, although some pupils had clearly misheard fingertips for armpits.

The instruction 'roll your sleeves up' came too late for those up to their necks in it, but not soon enough for those that need thirty extra minutes of precious lesson time to undo their frustratingly tight cuffs.

One young man asked how he could make the dough with flour but no butter, whilst another young gentleman, with the opposing problem, all butter no flour, was equally perplexed. Unlike Mateo, not being in the miracle business, I had no answers to give.

Worse was to follow. A calamitous decision on my part for even thinking pupils capable of beating milk and egg together, to form the binding agent for the dough, without getting into a spin due to excessive centrifugal force. What's more, how hard can it be to crack an egg? I could have laid an egg more expeditiously than it took the pupils to fish out shards of eggshell from the swirling, turbulent mix.

The dough, produced from combining the wet and dry ingredients, ranged in consistency from wetter than the boys' toilets flooded floor to drier than a dead dingo's donger. And the only thing at my disposal to help remedy the situation was an empty flour dredger and a wing and a prayer.

Mrs Prendergast was on hand to tell me of every deficiency, or excess, depending upon whether the pupil was less or more inclined to the 'my cup runneth over' approach, with the blame for the disparity placed fairly and squarely at my door. Humble apologies for not realising a quarter pint of milk in one household is akin to two pints in another, with eggs ranging in size from those supplied by Coturnix coturnix (quail) – you would if you'd seen them – to the corpulent, corporate Golden Lay goose.

The dough, once finally workable – a considerable feat demanding actual blood, sweat and tears – had to be pressed onto a baking tray in the circular shape of a pizza, using only the flat of the hand. This was in preparation for the application of passata (posh tomato sauce, well it sounds posh with Mrs P's pronunciation, although on the same pronunciation proviso, if bath is pronounced barth, ass would be pronounced–? Quite!)

For the lesser classroom mortals, untrained in the art of elocution and diction, a banal tube of smooth tomato puree had to do.

Not wishing to appear imbecilic on the 'you say passata, I say passato' tune, I did some research and found out that tomato puree is a product that has been industrially sieved, to remove all seeds and lumps, whereas passata has not.

In Italy, the Italians refer to passata (try to imagine the arm waving, drama and energy that goes with it) as passata, and its minor league cousin, tomato puree, as passata di pomodoro, managing to make a meal, even out of that one. You have to hand it to the Mediterraneans. However, one girl, suffering from a serious case of Englishness, started to sob, albeit in a discreet, dignified, and reserved manner, that her passata di pomodoro was 'faulty' because there was no response when she squeezed. Well, that won't be for the last time, I'm sure!

Once a breakthrough had been achieved (such a lot to learn in life), standard pizza toppings, such as home pre-chopped vegetables, rough or fine (as in the chopping action, not the background of the vegetable acceptable to Mrs Prendergast), home pre-chopped, pre-cooked meats and home grated cheese were added to the base, along with a surplus to requirements, tooth. Teething problems at every stage.

The addition of the toppings was influenced by the area of expertise that the pupils felt most at home with. These areas ranged from the high sided sixpence, surface area suitable for a cherry tomato, to the full, flat rectangular, occupying every square inch of the baking tray, all notion of the circular going out of the window (along with the pupil pencil case, it's some sort of game the pupils like to play). The full flat providing a base so thin that the toppings could naturally find daylight from above and below.

On top of that – or not, as some children hadn't the strength to open the clear plastic bags of toppings so lovingly prepared by mother (or father, stepparent, grandparent, foster parent, guardian, the lollipop lady, I mean who cares, other than it would be world war three if we didn't get the form of address correct) – others couldn't prise the lids off the little Tupperware tubs. A third group, not bound by the conventions of the twenty-four-hour clock, were meticulously and artfully arranging toppings, one piece of sweetcorn at a time. No need for the action replay. I belong to the rough and ready, 'throw it all together now' with rising voice, professionally one note down from the Munch scream, school of cookery.

The lesson, even with home preparation time, was insufficient to make, bake, wash up, tidy up and get the pupils to shut up (anyone would think we were learning Italian), plus retrieve a missing pencil case, three storeys below, within the hour.

Mrs Prendergast complained that I hadn't emphasised the oven buddy system enough – one child courteously holds the oven door open, allowing another to safely peer in and, if cooked, extract their creation. I regularly fantasise about the oven buddy system. One child opens the oven door and yes, I think you've got it!

Well, the pupils didn't need an oven buddy when I was given the status of new best friend (without any of the usual wailing and soul searching for a replacement). I was oven buddy to everybody there.

Without my personal intervention, my newfound chums (a change from being hated and the usual refrain 'anybody but her') were incapable of judging for themselves whether a pizza was past the point of no return and reluctant to remove it having had their fingers previously burnt.

Nonetheless, we left the room immaculate – you could

have eaten pizza off the floor, but by God I made sure it had all been picked up before Mrs P could run her critical eye over the scene of the crime.

For the settled plenary (my heart rate was still beating too fast) and reflection (I could actually see my face in the spotless sinks and so had done something correctly, at long last), I thought I would throw in, 'As an alternative to the homemade pizza experience, try ringing Domino's next time for the ultimate spicy, meat feast glory, the big pepperoni (sounds faintly lewd) three cheese rustic (vegetarian), passata (not, passata di pomodoro) still in the jar (vegan), eggshell free, dairy free (all flour no butter), gluten free (all butter no flour), allergen free (less dust in the atmosphere), off the floor, stress free pizza!'

Yours truly,

Beth

PS I could always call round with a piece.

Skating on Thin Ice

28.02.18

Dear Cassie,

I don't know why I complained about the state of the spelling in your text replies to my letters –it seems so inconsequential now – but you must remember that text speak is alien to me. Indeed, if it hadn't been for your predicament, and prolonged absence from school, I would never have succumbed to texting in the first place, but desperate times call for desperate measures.

I remember the start of the whole sorry process, when Stuart put the numbers I would need into my phone, an offspring's cast off, to practise and become proficient at a means of communication I had, for so long, held out against.

During my trial runs, Alex said that he didn't appreciate being sent an essay and that wasn't the point of texting. I thought it a rather good way of getting across to him the rules of good financial management.

I did manage brevity in my response to the first ever text Stuart sent me. Very romantic – 'Do we need more parsnips?' It makes you wonder just how many parsnips a family can go through over the Christmas period.

Meg said that it was all well and good; she's less in need of stringent fiscal control, though she does appreciate the nicely roasted parsnip, but added I would have to remember to keep my phone switched on. Well, that's easier said than done. Having a two-handed grip, perfected for the correct hoeing technique, has precluded my hand from mutating and evolving the permanent communications appendage. Not only that, but I'm so low down in the digital evolutionary chain that I haven't enough megabytes to even find it, the phone that is, not the other article that PSE are so fixated on, although I think that I could just about remember where to find that without having to mount a search party. That must be worth three cartwheels and a back flip, but I'll never be able to access the relevant emoji to represent it.

Nonetheless, despite my best efforts, I received an extremely poor end of term report on my telephone manner, with a plethora of areas highlighted for further development. In my defence, I would very much like to point out that we can't all be absorbed in a subject that leads us directly into the lamppost; I've never run with the pack. And I might not be adept with fastest finger first, verboseness of text, battery life and chargers, the ability to hear or even recognise one's own ring tone, and feeling the vibe, possibly the vibration, it could be either; but at least I haven't succumbed to the form of address favoured by the lodger and the PC, 'yo' from the former and 'hey guys' from the latter. I am not so Victorian as to expect dearest mama and papa, but I do think there should be a modicum of civility in their text introductions. Even you are not beyond approach, using the casual hi at the start of parental e-mail replies, despite my warning cries. But alas, from this point forward, I would accept any form of address from you, I'd take the 'hey hi ho yo' (it might catch on) over the correct and acceptable 'dear' so long as you could continue to get your message through.

I know that you have never been too keen on writing, your informal introductions exemplifying this, relying on the artist's get out clause, 'a picture paints a thousand words', but oh Cassie, the school e-mail is absolutely the saddest way to learn that you will never make a brush stroke again, having finally lost your stoic battle against lung cancer at the age of only forty-six.

We are told that you passed away peacefully, in your own home, surrounded by your loving family, and all I can think is why didn't I set up the science smoking machine in your classroom, every single lunch time, to demonstrate the dangers of inhaled nicotine and choking black tar. If I had, you might still be here; weaving your magic and making everyone who met you feel better for sharing your company, a true gift.

Bizarrely, in the face of the heart-breaking news, I find myself at my desk, utterly bereft, composing a letter that will never be read but one that I feel compelled to express.

I need you to know that you have been a dear friend and supportive colleague, and I have been enriched for knowing you and I don't use the word lightly, considering all its connotations; but it is true, you have lifted my spirits a thousand-fold or more, especially when I have needed support the most. I think back to my husband's own gruelling cancer treatment followed by a pulmonary embolism, blocking his lung, a life-threatening condition thrown in just for good measure.

Support was also on hand during my offspring's escapades and debacles; let's face it, namely Alex's debacles. My stock-in-trade advice of 'read the exam question carefully' is only beneficial if the person taking the exam, in this case at university, can be motivated to turn up for it. It had never occurred to me to say read the question carefully, in the actual examination room, as part and parcel of the effective examination technique.

And finally, there has been the tumult of teaching so many different subjects to unknown, often challenging classes at a minute's notice, chipping away mercilessly at my confidence, in the game of thirty against one. Classes that always sense that the supply teacher is on a hiding to nothing, particularly when neither exercise books, lined paper, textbooks, guidance notes for the lesson, the remote control for the interactive board, the window pole (for the closed window in summer and the open window in a snowstorm) or the light switch can be found, and take full advantage of the opportunities presented to them.

Departmental nomadic supply teaching is incredibly isolating, with no one willing to step in and fight your corner, the overburdened staff a little green eyed that, at the end of the day, the supply teacher can step away. And yet your door, not a jealous bone in sight, has always been open (perhaps a little more vigilance on that one considering the escalating thefts), giving reassurance and encouragement that the paper and exercise books will one day be found. Moreover, valuing and appreciating the work I carried out, complimenting, 'with you they know the drill', the highest it seems, without mention of any natural teaching skills, to which I can aspire.

Whatever life has thrown at me – although by a long chalk, the interactive board has helped on that score – you have been there for me, buoying me up when I have been down, always making me smile. 'If you didn't laugh, you'd cry', your mantra. Although, to be fair, some of us don't have the luxury of tears these days due to a tearless dry eye, the skin not the only organ to deteriorate under the fluorescent classroom lighting.

Yet, you could light up a classroom, not by a flow of electrons, but with kindness, consideration and compassion, attributes never to be forgotten, along with your quirky sense of humour and over the top tank tops, suitable for only an art teacher to wear. The teaching of chemistry and the mandatory lab coat does have the occasional merit. And a lab coat with extra deep pockets would certainly have come in handy at the last Parents' Evening, no pun intended, for when you had overdone it with the fake tan. Fewer pins and needles than having to sit on your hands the whole evening to avoid parents noticing hands and face didn't tally! Just one of a raft of treasured memories to look back upon with a smile as I think of your various scrapes.

From the outset of the diagnosis the outlook was poor, surgery not an option. As always, your concern was for others, especially your cherished sister and parents, and so you courageously, without rancour, fought the illness, determined to spend, and share Christmas with your adored family for one final time. And you made it, against all the odds, to a Christmas you thought out of reach.

I realised that the end was close when you had lost the strength to text, but it is human nature to never give up hope. I hope that I respected your wishes to not give the cancer airtime in my letters, but instead to bring normality, a contradiction in terms for the secondary school, to the fore.

You have been in my thoughts throughout and I hope, in the smallest of ways, I have managed to make you smile, and that you are laughing now, at the mortals you leave behind, at this precise moment in time, in imminent icicle danger.

'Beware falling icicles' declare the resource ladies and I can only assume the coffee dregs launching from the tower block windows are freezing in the bitter cold air before they hit the ground. Who would have thought that pressing a photocopying button could hold such perils?

I wish with all my heart that we could dodge the razor tipped icicles together, along with the snowballs, footballs, cricket balls, rugby balls and any other balls the pupils care to lob in our direction. There is always safety in numbers, and a trouble shared is a trouble halved, particularly if it helps with the deflection.

My message today, forget the word and thought of the week is, 'beware all pupils', for I have lost a precious friend and indefatigably brave colleague, so woe betide the pupil greeting me, with 'oh f....ing hell', followed by a glancing blow to the head.

Choppy Waters

24.10.18

Dear Cassie,

I have missed you dreadfully in the last eight months, devoid of your intuitive wit, insight, and perspective, but out of sight is not the same as out of mind. In my head, I find myself talking to you, very much as before, even though I know full well that there will never be a reply, in much the same vein as when you were alive; really a text is no substitute for the proper letter.

However, that doesn't mean to say you are not hearing me on some subliminal level and so after a period of silence and remembrance, I've decided to put pen to paper once more, for a process that will be cathartic for me, if not for you. This will allow me to garner my thoughts and find a way through (not the Ouija board, I don't believe in any of that nonsense), but everyday family life and the perils of school, trusting as always, you'll remain on my embattled and beleaguered side.

It is difficult to know where to begin, but to start the ball rolling, I am delighted to say that the PC has finally got onto the property ladder, leaving her apartment behind. As parents, we have spent the last couple of years explaining that renting an apartment is not the way to go, when all efforts should be put into acquiring bricks and mortar, but as with everything else in life, the PC will only do her own.

The house buying process has not been without challenge. The first house sought by the PC, a tiny terrace property in Lower Mill, a small town on the wrong side of the Pennines, was in a flood zone. How I rue, bucking the trend, that we didn't beget a 'gifted and talented'! It's not much good studying a geography degree, with modules on fluvial geomorphology and river management, if you can't spy, with the detective's eye, the road immediately outside the house, cordoned off for culvert repairs. It turns out that culvert isn't a physical geographical feature listed in the extensive glossary for fluvial geomorphology and river management, under flood!

Of course, if the PC had followed one of my mother's staunch pillars of life, she would have known, as naturally as breathing, to never live at the bottom of a hill, or in the valley bottom, but always, indeed absolutely always, to reside at the top. It is as fundamental to a successful life as learning times tables, having a dictionary to hand to unearth (a direct consequence of the flooding) the name of a covered water channel, not using batteries, maximising on all coupons and offers and being able to account for every penny spent in life. My dad thinks that the ledgers, going back to when Nellie the Elephant was trumpeting her stuff, could become museum pieces one day.

Anyway, when the house needing a boat was ruled out of the water by parents with a more critical understanding of current affairs, the PC directed her efforts to searching for a house in Upper Mill, the 'upper' satisfying the required elevation in my mother's rule book. The 'upper slopes' may also help the PC to capitalise on her claim that glaciers, ice sheets, permafrost and periglaciation are more her thing, although that remains to be seen.

The chalet, not a ski lift in sight, got as far as the survey stage even though Stuart and I hadn't had the opportunity to cast a critical eye due to prior holiday commitments. However, we should have known better than to leave the PC to her own devices. A retrograde step considering the curious incident of the PC and the battering ram, and one which should have presaged that structural engineering wasn't her forte. It's nothing short of a miracle that the PC and her colleague weren't sued, after the walls to either side of the door under bombardment collapsed, yet the door itself remained wilfully intact; goodness only knows what sort of cack-handed demolition techniques they were employing.

So, to cut a long story short, I said you can't possibly buy a house with a roof and four walls about to cave in; the battering ram should have been deployed before shelling out for a costly surveyor's report. It's no-good complaining to me about the wasted expense when pointing (mortar, not fingers) and tingles (S-shaped metal clips to support roofing slates, not sensations) are in the dictionary blind spot. If the PC doesn't up her vocabulary game soon, my mother will never be knocked off the family games top spot. Mind you, I will be able to contribute a 'parliament of crows' to the quiz, since finding out that the unstable, uncapped chimney, had more crows, possibly rooks, than school yard shitting seagulls.

Third time lucky, Stu and I were purposefully on hand to interrogate the estate agent, a young man with small tattoo on his neck, desperately in need of the 1970s polo jumper (I never thought it would find a use), to ascertain whether either Noah or the three little pigs with various roofing options, were needed to seal the roof.

Consequently, it has been a stressful process for many reasons but an alpine mid terrace, in sound order – every expletive vented next door – with contemporary fixtures and fittings has finally fulfilled all requirements. Indeed, it has exceeded all requirements and if an address incorporating the words Mount Pleasant doesn't bestow praise from my mother, for having reached the pinnacle of acceptability, then quite frankly, nothing will.

School, it transpires, is not burdened with delivery dates and time slots – 'Can you come across, Mum, it is imperative that someone is in between seven am and seven pm, when I'm (possibly deliberately) on duty?' to accept all the goods needed to make a house into a home. No, the school is dealing with matters of international importance, not fending off phone calls from 'wasting away' husbands distressed that the tea is not on the table.

Startling revelations that that the school needed to get its own house in order were brought to the fore by the head of history, suddenly finding himself propelled into the midst of a political dust storm. He has unwittingly stumbled across a set of car keys 'lurking' in the history office. No ordinary find because the keys, menacingly, were accompanied by a skull and Soviet Union key fob. The head of history, spooked by the discovery, has released a statement to say that he will not be commenting on recent international events.

Believe you me, my family can give international events a run for their money when the tea is behind schedule and the Next sofa won't fit through either the front or the back door, and I am told by the delivery men 'We'll come back, within a twelve-hour time slot, when you have arranged to take the front window out'. Compared to that seismic event (another geographical specialism not fully grasped due to the lack of a tape measure), the school, even with the Ruskies amongst us, has got off lightly. I always knew the boiled cabbage soup would have its ramifications.

Not to be outdone by the history department's impressive find, specialist area of interest, the Cold War (I'm sure there is a legal requirement to provide classroom heaters when the temperature drops to Siberian levels), the resource ladies, to balance their unremitting losses have gained a set of keys with 'Wallace and Gromit'. Wallace and Gromit, they want to thank their lucky stars, some people are dealing with 'Lenin and Trotsky'.

'Wallace and Gromit', we are pointedly and reliably informed, 'were left on the counter' in resources. In accordance with the punishment should fit the crime, it will be nothing less than the gulag for the perpetrator of that indiscretion when found. Furthermore, the ladies wish to track down who has lost a lens from their reading glasses (they think the person would know), because 'one' has been 'left on the counter'.

Someone is clearly dicing with death in the 'dare to leave

it on the counter' game and I'd rather brave an irate husband not served his tea in the designated ten-minute slot, five minutes either side of five o'clock, than be in further hot water with the resource department on the trail of the Monocled Mutineer.

The pupil receptionist of the day (a runner with younger, fitter, more energetic legs than those of the sedentary school secretaries – a fixed position) has also been handing out messages. The messages, delivered in tandem with boot bags, planners, keys, coats, bus passes, lunch boxes and half size cellos that have become accidently or deliberately separated from their rightful owners, have varied in threat level. Low grade security messages have been along the lines of 'Please tell Ebony White to collect her ostrich egg (– I knew it!) from the science lab where it has been left', or 'Can all pupils attending animal care (crucifixion more like) please be allowed to leave for college five minutes early'. However, not all the messages have been for public consumption.

One day last week, the 'pupil runner of the day', looking less appealing than the soup, cannoned through the maths room door, at twenty-five minutes past three, panting and clutching a note to his chest, shouting out between laboured breaths, 'Is this Mr Fitzsimmons' classroom?' I replied that it was, keeping Mr Fitzsimmons' alias, Mr Findlater, a guarded secret. Walls have ears. The pupil receptionist of the day then demanded, 'Are you Mr Fitzsimmons?' I did not deign the question with a reply but merely gave the look and said curtly, 'Pass me the note.'

'I can't do that,' replied the emboldened, cocky pupil with

upgraded security clearance. 'I can only give this extremely important and urgent message, which must be read out before three thirty (stand back for the grand school bus depart) to the teachers on my list and if you are not Mr Fitzsimmons, you are not on the list.' Not to put too fine a point on it, doesn't that just sum up the story of my entire supply teaching career.

Yours truly

Beth

Taken for a Mug

03.11.18

Dear Cassie,

It comes as no surprise to me that the present-day teenager is conflicted considering the mixed messages handed out by the school.

Word of the Week – Scrumptious: adjective – delightful, delicious.

Thought of the Week – Knowledge is the food of the soul.

Instruction of the Week – apprehend any pupil seen leaving the dining room, at morning breakfast club, with hot chocolate in hand.

Genius Thought of the Week – Food and Drink must not leave the dining room, or better still, form any part of the dining arrangements!

Considering the state of the dining room floor at lunchtime, a total moratorium on all food and drink is the only answer to the dinner ladies' prayers.

A fledgling female teaching assistant, uninitiated in the art of keeping everything you own within clear sight, has radioed for help following the disappearance of her thermos flask, a Stainless-Steel King in racing green, with 'coffee still in it'! I doubt that very much. Not with hot chocolate 'nil by mouth'.

The ladies in the school office need a Chubb Battleship Padlock, not the trophy cabinet key, to secure their survival provisions. Their entire supply of Dairy Pride semi-skimmed long-life milk, all eight cartons, plus an English fine bone china mug – no indecent image (some people have more class) – belonging to the school secretary, has been taken. The office ladies are appealing for witnesses and have made a heartfelt plea to the callous thief or thieves to replenish their stocks. There is less hope for the return of the English fine bone china mug. It is not the type of mug the police regularly find when cross-checking the inventory at the pawn shop.

The hard-pressed (there's more than one action to expertly master) resource ladies have lost the 'silver trolley'. 'Silver trolley!' You may well gasp. The poor old school governors can't get hold of a biodegradable, compostable, recyclable paper straw in barber shop colours let alone 'summon' the butler for waiter service. Have you ever known such an eclectic collection?

Mrs Drinkwater has lost the Christmas Fair Banner, nothing unusual there. Only this time, it wasn't lost from the small store cupboard, the choice of plunder, but from the school gates, where she had tied it most securely. And it looks like we will all be spending the month of December with 'fingers on lips' because the 'Silence Exams in Progress' signs have disappeared in mock exam season. I don't know why anyone should be surprised; it is coming up to Christmas and some people do like to grab the more unusual gift.

The jazz band won't have to face the music over their usual breach of the peace because they have lost their Christmas Cheer. A red box of Christmas cheer, housing the Christmas jazz band musical notation. It could potentially be 'anywhere in school'. Look on the bright side: no one will be urgently dispatched to the music room door, holding up a reminder, 'Silence Exams in Progress'.

Racing Billy is certainly getting into the Christmas spirit early, with or without the band, and dressing very seriously for the occasion. Nothing but his best bib and tucker, in fact, for the upcoming Christmas Variety Show. Racing Billy desires anything 'Christmassy' that can be worn to dress people up in (each to their own) including hats and slippers, with lots of twinkle, but cautions against anything rude. Makes you wonder what sort of bed hat and slippers the guy normally wears!

Mind you, Billy's needs are small fry compared to Props Honeypots gearing up for the next school production of Oliver. 'Please, Sir, I want some more.' That would be more in terms of a small cat or dog (his ambitions know no bounds) basket. A candlestick (or two), 'in your face, over the top' Liberace style bling. Plastic fruit (a refreshing change from the usual five a day mantra), four small milk churns (with or without eight cartons of Dairy Pride long-life semi-skimmed milk) and/ or matching galvanised buckets. He would also like a pocket watch (no need for rehearsals, they know how to pick a pocket or two), wicker flower baskets and frilly umbrellas. I think the word he is looking for there is parasol but the man will try any way he can to slip 'frilly' naturally into the conversation.

I give him better odds for the Liberace look than the head of science anxiously searching for anyone with a cowbell 'hanging around', possibly left over from the Tour de France. She needs the cowbells, the more the better, for the STEM (science, technology, engineering, and mathematics) Club challenge along with seven paddling pool pumps. As with Racing Billy, whatever floats your boat.

The science department is also looking for donations (it's a very precise figure) of one hundred and fifty drawing pins. No mention is made of their intended use, but as pin the tail on the donkey has gone out of fashion I'm left wondering if pin the 'hanging about cowbell' to the cow's neck beckons as an idea for the latest enrichment lesson, either that or one hundred and fifty ways to deflate your paddling pool. But who am I to say, I'm only the 'don't count' (certainly not on this occasion) supply teacher.

In other school developments credence has finally been given to my theory that 'It was the magic fairies that did it, guv'. Confirmation of magic fairies working in school has been confirmed by way of the school's recycling policy. The magic fairies, evidently, will not be 'flattening' the cardboard boxes dumped in the parcel room. These must be 'flattened' by our good selves. Willingly, but I didn't think, under restorative justice policy, the practice was still allowed. And the magic fairies won't be visiting classrooms either to collect the recycling boxes. According to Big Mac, who seems to be something of an authority on the magic fairy, it is the responsibility of form monitors to collect and stack the recycling boxes correctly. And form teachers, who are ultimately responsible for the process, need to oversee operations. Seemingly, all teaching staff over the age of thirty-three will be dead and buried before wasteful recycling has had an impact.

You're telling me, and I for one don't want to be found 'dead and buried' under a mound of incorrectly stacked papers with a manslaughter prosecution looming for the pupil. Far less risk to all concerned if the pupils take some of it home, in a 'flattened' cardboard box, to help with efficient distribution.

In plain sight, Props Honeypots has made a last-minute appeal to add to his original list of props for 'Oliver' and put out a request for a 'hip flask'. I know, it is unbelievable, but he gets away with it. No wonder he needs an inflatable bed to lie down on after a little tipple, considering what to do with his 'frillies'.

Mr Honeyman's interest in ornithology (I am surprised the man can find the time), continues unabated but this time, rather than feathers to tickle your fancy, he requires 'a small stuffed bird (sparrow sized). Can you oblige?'

Pity he didn't want it, some years back, when I had to teach a food technology Christmas lesson on how to make a chocolate log that left me spitting feathers. When I say 'make', I do not want to give the impression that the children were toiling away, trying to tightly roll a freshly baked sponge without cracking. I mean that their parents had to supply a readymade Swiss Roll in preparation for the glories of the 'in school' chocolate butter cream making experience, lesson plan title, 'How thick can you smother it', with embellishments. The embellishments could include decorations made from fondant icing, such as holly leaves and red berries, silver beads, chocolate buttons, sprinkles and so forth, along with small, hygienically clean, festive novelties. Very artistic, just your sort of thing, 'moins le glitter'.

One boy achieved a successful learning outcome without any of the prescribed learning. Pitching up with a fully decorated, shop bought Yuletide log, commensurate to the beating process, that is of the icing sugar, margarine, and chocolate powder, not the boy for failing to listen carefully, but how I so wish, with 'We Wish You a Merry Christmas' sign in silver lettering, didn't deter from the layering process. Not wishing to spoil the ship for a ha'porth of tar can be taken too far and there must be a legal limit on butter cream to cake ratio before a teenager barfs.

I suppose I should be grateful that the silver 'We Wish You a Merry Christmas' sign had a more seasonal feel to it than 'Congratulations on your 21st Birthday'. Alas, I wouldn't have screamed if my vision hadn't been impaired by plumes of icing sugar, spiralling into the atmosphere on a par with a Polar vortex during the frosting process, but I was hardly expecting to see a fully fledged bird, feather deep in butter cream, glassy eyed, impassively staring up to icing sugar heaven. A small, plastic, hygienically clean novelty is not a life-size, taxidermy stuffed robin designed to hang from the branch of an eight-foot Norwegian spruce.

However, if Props Honeypots really is looking for the

'small, stuffed bird, sparrow sized', I think I know the relevant department to oblige!

Yours truly

Beth

PS From now on I will be making fairy cakes only.

Driven to Distraction

30.12.18

Dear Cassie,

I am very aware that this is the first Christmas your family and friends have not had the joy of your company and I know how much you will have been missed. Forgive me, therefore, for launching straight into my own Christmas tale, a defence strategy, to bolster my own resolve in your absence and prevent me from dwelling on my own immeasurable sadness.

Well, where to start the dissection on another year of family Christmas festivities, once again, held at my sister's home (I'm not sure if she is a saint or a glutton for punishment), in North Yorkshire.

The PC certainly lowered the tone over the full family dinner table with tales of her bestiality arrest. I said, 'Surely that can wait until after we've eaten,' but my nieces and nephews (my brother and sister both managed to copy my idea of a boy first and a girl second – you can hardly put your arm over that sort of work), were all agog and their eyes drawn momentarily from the pigs in blankets surveillance, allowing the lodger to unobtrusively dive in to get an advantaged share.

After a full, literally, blow by blow, account of the case, I felt vindicated that my long-held view, 'a lick is worse than a bite', had finally come to fruition.

My mother remarked, with considerable distaste, that seven pups a licking hardly had the same ring to it as seven swans a laying but my nephews, less concerned with the morals of a voyeuristic partridge, were more interested in what the lady (I use the term loosely) in the case had used 'down below' to encourage the pups in their activities.

I ventured I hardly thought that she'd had a can of Chum up there but that just led to the opening up of another can of worms. In fact, you would be surprised to learn that you don't always need a bag for life to carry your shopping home in. You can't say that the criminal underworld is not doing its bit for plastic reduction targets. I bet no one thought to look up there for the cherry jelly, hormone rooting powder, and a small pair of yellow fibreglass step ladders, although the latter could be considered a stretch too far. I would have asked the orifice oracle about this possibility but feared being turned into stone, a genetic trait, inherited initially from my mother's mother, and passed on with considerable success down the female line.

As it happens, six mobiles phones, not a pair of step ladders, found on a male suspect, seems to be the record for amazing storage capacity, for those given pertinent facts on the strip search course. Although it is hardly the course certification a normal person would wish to have emblazoned on the curriculum vitae.

Pity those with a penchant for puppies didn't think to hide their own phone up the jacksie, as some of the indecent images were sufficient in nature to turn Sarge, in-house parlance for the sergeant to you and me, green.

My father, who is a stickler for hygiene when it comes to food preparation, on a par matched only by Mrs P, commented that he hoped that the PC had washed her hands thoroughly before passing him the roast parsnips, but one of my nieces, now working in the field of human rights was only concerned with the welfare of the pups. Well, on that score we can all breathe a sigh of relief because they have been taken into puppy care.

Hubby, one photographic course under his belt, was less concerned with the pups' removal and being taken into care, than on how the actual filming had been done and at what angle. I just gave the look; the PC is not the only one capable of petrifaction. Rest assured: it is not something he ever need worry about in the pursuit of artistic licence. I volunteered I doubted it could have been a selfie. Lacking an arboreal limb, I am incapable of even taking a face selfie, so how the woman in question managed to keep a steady hand during the tickling process, for want of a better description, I have no idea. However, the PC, who is becoming increasingly worldly wise, in all matters except the geographical – nobody likes a know-all – with a scornful look to indicate 'don't be so stupid', made the point that a camera would have been set up to capture the action.

When my brother (he who shall be saveth the lion's share of the roast potatoes with lashings of gravy – the joy of the pride) asked if the suspect was dog rough or simply barking, the PC countered that she hadn't managed to get Christmas Day off to take a busman's holiday and could we all kindly change the subject.

That was a bummer because it gave my mother the opportunity to hold court, regaling her captured audience with cruise ship talk. Who my parents had sat by at breakfast, elevenses, lunch, afternoon tea, dinner, and supper (how the devil do those cruise liners stay afloat?), who had said what to whom, who had notched up the most cruises, was annoying, boring, boastful, wonderful, intelligent, not so sharp, loud, didn't speak up loud enough, overweight – hardly a surprise if we had only been there to examine the troughing habits of the people impossible to see under their own piled high food plates. Clearly my parents have been sailing aboard the Latino cruise liner, 'The Miss McDonald'. It is at times like this that I pray the pigs in blanket stack isn't going to spectacularly collapse, due to undermining at its base, with the blame for greed fairly and squarely pointed at poor parenting techniques.

The cruise ship conversation is all very well (conversation being a stretch greater than those trying to accommodate a pair of small, yellow fibreglass steps), more of a recant on one side and a glazing over on the other. And whatever the merits of the entertainment it is hardly likely to live up to the antics of the magnificent seven.

Only cruise ship talk can make me want to participate in the dreaded Christmas family quiz. I thought Windsor was quite a good answer to a 'chair you would sit in by the fireside'.

I know Windsor is in Berkshire, not Yorkshire, even though the quiz was on clues about Yorkshire towns, but it was the only chair I could think of and thought it better than leaving a blank. After all, we tell our charges often enough to never leave a question blank. Anyhow, as you are not of cruise ship age, along with the rest of us bar two, I will put you out of your misery – the answer is Settle. I am not surprised my mother continues her eighty odd years winning streak; she is at a distinct advantage.

I sincerely hope that the PC will never have to solve any cryptic clues to solve a case or else she will be rocking up to the scene of the crime at the town of 'Gone off' (there are some for whom the blank should always be the default position), for the clue 'out of date', rather than Selby, but then again she is seriously geographically challenged.

After the quiz came my mother's surprise Christmas presents. The boys, as in son, sons-in-law and grandsons, were told there would be no surprise this year as socks, quite frankly, were boring and no one seemed to appreciate them. My mother has very selective powers of perception. The girls, however, as in daughters, daughter-in-law and granddaughters could still be surprised by the annual scarf and magnetic 'To Do' pad for attachment to the fridge. I wonder what a psychologist would make of over fifty years' worth of annual 'To Do' pads (idle hands lead to idle minds). There's no rest for the wicked when there is always a home, not a school, list to hand.

I was inwardly commending myself on our inspired gift to the PC when the person in question piped up, in contemptuous tone, to a full audience, 'You'll never credit what my parents have got me for Christmas'. Staggeringly, an outdoor security light, even one we had managed to wire up and get working (in secret whilst she was on duty) before the PC moved into her new house has fallen short in the exciting surprise Christmas gift stakes and has gone down like a pair of annual Christmas socks weighted with a portion of my sister's homemade self congratulatory Christmas Pud.

Word of the Week – Smug: adjective – the ability to make one's own Christmas Pudding. The result of an annual evening event spent with the girls – five middle aged fifty-somethings, breaching the age trades description act, sharing the plumpest middle-class sultanas, not the typical dried up, wizened little shrivels, 'lurking' out of date, in the standard kitchen cupboard, along with other pooled, brandy doused, fine ingredients, to mitigate costs. That 'the girls' partake in the batch baking process with champers, for themselves, not the inebriated pud, and that the husbands are despatched en mass to the nearest hostelry, has no bearing on keeping the overall production costs down.

Anyway, I digress, we had been commending ourselves on such an illuminating present, but all I can say is that it failed to light the PC's face up. You would think that someone in the security business would be more appreciative of such a carefully thought out and useful present, but alas not when she was hoping for: a bottle of Jo Malone. A puff of Jo Malone in the burglar's eye would be a very costly deterrent.

However, if ever you find yourself acting as an outdoor lighting electrician for the great heavenly skies, don't leave the kitchen window, next to where you have been working, wide open, and then drive away, as the new floodlight will simply show any potential burglars the way forward. Believe you me, our ears are still ringing and that is before we have even begun our amateur efforts with the installation of a DIY wireless home security system.

The lodger, not to be outdone in the cruellest Christmas presents a parent could have ever given their child, brought out his old and long-standing grievance chestnut of the times table box. How simply ungrateful can offspring be? He should consider himself extremely fortunate that a thoughtful aid had been provided to help him master one of my mother's cornerstones of life without the need for rote. If he had successfully learnt his tables by the designated age of six, we would not have had recourse to buy a times table box at the age of seven to help him on his way. And as for the wok given at age seventeen, another monumental flop, but a computer game is hardly going to cook a meal in preparation for university.

After Christmas came the sales and without sight nor sound of a potential husband for the PC, or a wedding that presumably would have generated wedding present gifts in abundance, it transpired that I had been left to fill the gap in the home furnishings department for her new house. I think it is fair to say that my single contribution to Dunelm Mills has seen their profits soar this year. However, the journey to the store on the Lancashire side (do you know how many lanes of traffic need to be negotiated in Ashton-under-Lyne?) had to be undertaken as a passenger, and my strict criteria for remaining silent not met. It is frustrating that my husband tends to drive at 'twenty to four' rather than 'ten to two,' as my driving instructor expressly instructed thirty-eight years ago and from which I have not deviated since; but when an officer of the law is casually holding on to the wheel at half past six, it is impossible to silence the scream. Stationary traffic is no excuse, one should always be ready for the off.

Next time I encounter a pupil jumping uncontrollably out of their seat, with no sign of crossing their legs, I will, from now on, for a good second at least, give credence to a nervous disposition and try a generally more empathetic approach.

Yours truly

Beth

Standing on Ceremony

12.01.19

Dear Cassie,

As if the January sales rollercoaster ride hasn't been enough to test the limits of my survival (we were practically on blue lights to grab the bargain – the generational practice deeply ingrained in the mitochondrial DNA), tackling the month's other obligatory task, booking holidays for the year, has proved equally taxing.

I thought that I would start the process with our twice-yearly trip, May and October, to the Lake District, and get our bed and breakfast accommodation sorted out for the first of these two sojourns at the May Day Bank Holiday. Having stayed at the same pub for the last fifteen years, I was taken aback when the manager taking the booking said, 'Are you aware of our new breakfast policy?' I replied that I was not but thought to myself that I would be able to cope with anything other than the previously endured 'lite bite' fiasco.

Well, you could have knocked me down with a feather, along with any other light headed guests sorry enough to be subjected to the new breakfast policy – a policy withdrawing the most important meal of the day. Who wants to sign up for the bed only experience, misery really does make strange bedfellows?

Hubby was quick to find a motel at Lancaster, on the Lakeland periphery, as an alternative source of accommodation. He always goes for the cheaper outskirts and commented 'picky' when given 'the look' for pointing out I need 'the works', not something inedible wrapped in cellophane, to get the day started.

The lodger (it is impossible to have any sort of private conversation since he moved back home without receiving unsolicited advice) said that with my 'bmi' rating, cellophane would be more health conducive than a daily cholesterol shot, and I really should be restricting myself to carrots and lettuce. You would think I was a rabbit, not his mother, although the bastard bunnies breaking and entering the garden are not restricting the calories. Have you any idea of the cost of chicken wire, which comes only with wire, not the chick? I could enjoy bed, breakfast, and a three-course evening meal for the price of mounting 'The Bunnies Beware' rabbit fortification.

There was little in the way of sympathy from those that can't tell the time with a steering wheel but this was more to do with my reaction to the 'snuggle' seating for the new home, than the ability to remain a passive passenger.

The snuggle, the cleverest marketing term ever, is an anathema to me and can only be described as a modern-day chair that is too big for one person or a sofa that is too small for two, but perfectly proportioned for the male orangutan. Whatever, it is a piece of furniture that needs to come with a built-in chiropractor. I remarked, 'Your father and I can't sit in this; we're on a twist', but that got the response we needed to relax, loosen up, and get with it. Being superglued to the steering wheel at ten to two for nearly forty years hardly helps with flexibility. I don't know about get with it, I couldn't even get fully on it, and don't consider having one arse cheek perked up in the air ergonomically satisfactory.

The three-seater settee, reduced to a two-seater, after the failed delivery attempt and my refusal to contemplate sitting in a draught for a twelve-hour period, wasn't an option, as we had taken my parents to see the PC's new home and believe you me my parents can move at the speed of the police car when they have to. They like their creature comforts, although, benevolently, were prepared to sit at either end, to allow 'Numero Uno' to squeeze between them. My mother was in her Italian phase; having lessons to learn the language, not produce the essence of the classic margherita, when the lodger was born and so forever more, as the first grandchild, he has been granted this title.

I thought it rather presumptuous that my parents thought they could sit on the brand-new sofa, a serious breach of their own sofa rules.

As a teenager, when my parents got a Bridgecraft, the Rolls-Royce of the deluxe three-piece suite, and more revered than the full Hornsea Pottery Dinner Set, I had to admire it from the position of the floor, utmost of three years.

The superior Bridgecraft didn't masquerade as a 'snuggle', or even worse, in the words of a clearly deluded delivery driver, a 'love seat'. I don't expect to be asked to sign for a 'love seat' at my age, although I suppose anything that helps the PC's cause. In my day it was levitation, not loving, that was expected of a quality Dralon; no wonder it was built to last.

The PC and I (note – not me and the PC – for all pupils that do not pay attention in English) had artfully dressed the new snuggles (the two-seater could technically be classed as snug for the three persons) but the insouciant house guests tossed aside the carefully coordinated accessories, in a bid to make space, without putting so much as a hand up to ask permission.

My husband would have to be genetically modified to appreciate the cushion and is as antagonistic and irrational towards the bed valance as a seven-year-old towards the 'My times table box'. What's more, he is far too fond of saying, 'mark my words, the valance would be the first thing to go'. Yes well, if he coddles the valance under the mattress one more time, to get to the drawer under the bed, he may find that he has gone before the valance. The man needs counselling for boudoir cushion and bed runner rage and a course of intensive therapy if he is ever to learn how to spruce.

For her first house guests' entertainment, not to be outdone by her auntie's dog's appearance on the Yorkshire Vet, the PC produced a recorded episode of Bargain Hunt, in which two of her closest friends were participating. Knowing actual people as opposed to a one-eyed dog gives greater insight into the production of the programme.

As we all sat round to watch, some more comfortably than others, we were given the insider knowledge that Philip Serrell, one of the antique experts, is something of an acquired taste. A little bit like the 'snuggle' then.

My parents, quite indignantly, commented that they didn't like Philip Serrell whatsoever (harsh) because he had gone off with Paul Martin's (Flog It fame) trademark scarf, leaving lovely poor Paul Martin, scarf icon extraordinaire, scarf-less. I just don't know where they get their insider information from but as the PC's ears didn't prick up, I don't think she will be taking up the case.

Numero Uno said he didn't care if it was man's best friend or the PC's best friend, he was not watching such shit (he's been far too influenced by his father's stance on soft furnishings), but multilingual mother suggested, if he was going to be uncouth, at least go for 'merda' to show some exercising of the brain. I doubt the neurotransmitters felt so much as a flicker and father and son probably thought they had been granted Scottish approval to commit a heinous crime on a cushion, not learn Italian shit.

So, due to a lack of interest in anything to adorn a house with, antique or new, the TV was ditched in favour of musical entertainment – not my mother's rendition of Albert and the Lion or, her alternative party piece, Meg Merrilies, and Meg's namesake, by Keats.

But music didn't calm the troubled waters, especially when the PC commanded her new gadget (sadly, not a stiff bristled yard broom), named 'Alexa', to play 'Adele'.

You don't have to get off your backside to set the music going with Alexa, a necessity for those wedged in the snuggle. I thought this a good thing although I wouldn't want to risk the command 'Beam me up Scottie'. However, Numero

Uno was scathing, on a scale of resentment reserved for the cushion, accusing the CIA of using Alexa as a listening device. And didn't the PC know everything left a trail, from mobile phones to social media.

My mother concurred – they share the conspiracy gene (originally inherited from my granddad who sadly died in 1965 but ahead of the game with his death bed warning, 'Beware of the Chinese' – he needn't have worried on my behalf, a woman on probiotics) – advising to keep off 'snapshot' and every other form of social media, detrimental to the decline of society and the world as we know it, and all because, as my mother loves to point out, people are simply incapable of keeping their thoughts to themselves.

Furthermore, my mother didn't want anybody listening in on her conversations (I know the feeling) and was vexed when Numero Uno said that keywords triggered the listening in process. Alas, I felt sorry for the poor bugger that got the 'cruise' trigger, mistaking cruise ship for cruise missile, and thought we should all remember, there are trickier jobs than teaching, although, admittedly, not very many.

Yours truly

Beth

PS I have been giving some thought to the lost, found, stolen, and suspended (pupils, not chairs) and concluded that as you are no longer able to help there is no point in continuing to highlight these areas. As such, in future correspondence, I will be turning my attention to lessons of the classroom, all topics equally morose. To save total parental embarrassment, alias names only, not the redacted X, will be used.

If the Cap Fits

14.02.19

Dear Cassie,

Have you any idea how embarrassing (although according to the PC, not as embarrassing as having your own mother teach you sex education in school) it is to start a Year 11 English lesson subjected to the words 'I hear you have got a cock in your garden, Miss, is it a big one?'

The long, stern, over the top of the reading glasses look, without flinch or recoil was needed to counter that one. I could hardly give a verbal response when I hadn't had a ruler to hand (they're all on loan, with penalty notices issued), to measure the size of the incursion; moreover, it is not something you expect to see before breakfast, proudly strutting its stuff.

How the class got wind of my early morning visitation, before the school day had begun, I have no idea. But believe you me: I was like a dog out of the traps, straight down the road to my neighbours, to see if they were missing one of their flock, more of the hen than the cock variety.

However, with biological observation skills in sharp decline, it is no good telling that to the gleeful teenage boy, with an affliction to enunciate 'cock' repeatedly, and a lascivious look to suggest he was proud enough to do a 'show and tell' on the spot.

So, back to my 'It's a Good Life' type neighbours. Instead of getting a straightforward yes, we are guilty, one of our hens has escaped to gorge on your free bird food (along with old Nutkins and his gang), I was asked for a description of the bird. A response that sums up the world in a nutshell: from fowl owners to jelly junkies, no one will acknowledge accountability anymore.

Thus, using all the descriptive powers I could muster, as befitting a 'stand in' English teacher for the day, I responded with, 'It looks like a hen', to help narrow down the list of suspects. I'm not suitably qualified to state, with absolute certainty, IC 3 female, possibly pullet.

However, 'hen' was not sufficiently descriptive (repeat the exercise) and the quizzing ratcheted up a notch to 'What colour of hen?'. I replied, 'bog standard', not realising that 'Miss Poultry' had made it onto the Farrow and Ball colour chart, 'Chic Chick with a hint of apple sauce' if I could get my hands on it.

Surely, a simple head count is all that is required (no need for the literal interpretation 'don't count your chickens'), followed by speedy retrieval, gracious apology, small reimbursement and sincere promise to remove the 'merda' defiling my lawn. We do have 'A Cut above the Rest', professional, four times yearly, lawn treatment, after all. There's no moss in my lawn, as those daring to lift their heads above the parapet, from the state-of-the-art trenches below will know.

However, I was met with polite indifference and had my wings clipped, if not the offender, with the suggestion that the culprit may be someone else's bird, no names given but hen honour respected in the 'right to roam'. In the face of such brazen, barefaced cheek and with the family insider knowledge, 'they never grass', I shall be mounting a fight back, using the tried and tested method, the fluorescent highlighter pen, to see how that puts a glowing cock (forget the cat) amongst the pigeons to tease out the rightful owner.

The rest of the school day didn't get much better, with repeated salutations of 'cock a doodle do, cock a doodle do' at every turn, and chicken dance impersonations (the chicken tonight advert really has reached its target audience) along with an overly enthusiastic interest in what I would be having for my tea.

The answers to the persuasive English writing task also left a lot to be desired. There's something to be said for teaching a subject that doesn't rely on the written word, even if a psychoanalyst does come in handy now and then. I wish that I had your professionalism to never wince.

Nonetheless, I thought that I would share with you a selection of some of the persuasive answers the pupils gave to a statement that had to be argued either, for or against, to show you what you have been missing out on all these years.

The statement read:

'Health clubs/ leisure centres/supermarkets/DIY stores/ pubs are more important than churches.

Answers:

1. Pubs are more important than churches because it is

better for the alcoholic to be in the pub than out on the street.

2. You need supermarkets to live because you can't get food from a church.

3. Church is only important to Christians who need it but you can't get fit there. Health clubs have a full fitness suite.

4. It is a lot more interesting at B & Q than sitting through a church service because you don't have to sing hymns or do the Lord's Prayer, but it can be busy on a Saturday.

5. I won the 200 metres breaststroke at my swimming club and my coach says I'm good enough for county level and I think this will get me a lot further in life than going to church. I have lots of cups and medals and I have had my name engraved on my best silver trophy.

6. I think it is important to keep fit because in the olden days children were made to go to church, but they weren't fit because there weren't any gyms.

7. Blank

If that sample choice doesn't make you feel grateful for your subject choice, nothing will. As for number 7, the 'least said, soonest mended' persuasive technique; the pupil had a waiver in the form of a parental note:

Teacher, a close family friend has died, and our dog of ten years is very poorly. Children gutted.

Parent

PS You can ring if you want.

Marking answers is a veritable minefield especially when tackling one of teaching's most perplexing mysteries, the multiple-choice paper.

What part of 'underline either A, B or C only' do you think it is that is baffling pupils? Some, with a strong betting instinct, underline all three, others with less confidence hedge their bets with two out of the three, whilst a third group fail to place any bets at all, poorly dogs excepting. Worst of all are the pupils that decide to write out the answer in full, without any sign of the A, B or C to speed up the marking process, meaning that I have to look back to see if the sentence given corresponds with the correct letter.

What is truly annoying and time consuming is the pupil who chooses to come up with an alternative to those presented in the multiple choice, taking the concept of multiple choice to new heights. It's not a free for all for anyone to put their penny worth in, even if the three choices in the sex and relationships assessment proved insufficient for one girl.

Question – A diaphragm or 'cap' needs to be placed:

A. Over the woman's cervix

B. In the opening of the vagina

C. Just inside the vagina

Answer – I think it should be put by the vagina.

I rest my case.

The second half of the assessment required full written answers but was equally challenging to award marks to, especially for those still operating in alphabet mode.

Question – how would you persuade your partner to use contraception?

Answer – C

More marks were available, or should have been, for the

longer, in depth answer, but where is the gifted, talented genius when one is needed?

Question – Describe a negative consequence of having sex with someone at an early age or the wrong person.

Answer – You might get the wrong person if you are drunk or wear glasses. Your youth may have gone. (I'm not capped, probably scarpered as soon as he'd sobered up and focused.)

Question – How are most sexually transmitted infections treated?

Answer – Paracetamol

Question – A condom is 98 percent reliable if used properly. Describe ways in which it can be made less reliable.

Answer – Throw it away after you have used it a couple of times (I see the problem, Big Mac – more work needed on sustainable recycling) and don't blow it up first (Gross).

Question – Where would a young person get free and confidential advice on contraception or sexual health?

Answer – The garage. (How to tell my mother – she thinks that barbecue coals look out of place.)

Nonetheless, I must stress vehemently, that I prefer marking the pupils' written answers to the pupils testing me for a verbal response to their questions. Despite all the advances in the field of education, and the many varied and progressive learning strategies, PSE still relies upon the old 'write a question down in secret' box to answer the pupils' concerns.

Question – What is anul sex? How I decry the demise of the weekly spelling list.

Question – How often do people have sex? (Every half

term if they teach in a secondary school but then again, not everyone is lucky enough to share the holiday timetable.)

Another glory you have missed out upon – you really should have got out of the art room more – is the PE department's fitness suite. It needs more than the Church and the power of prayer to withstand to work in that torture chamber, officiating Year 11 girls' fitness, with the equipment so heavily under strain. There are still some very meaty girls regardless of social media.

As you know, I usually refuse to teach PE lessons, still traumatised by my own as a child, but I was assured there were no rounders bats, hockey sticks, cricket balls or other offensive weapons in the fitness suite to inflict damage.

A further sweetener was given in the form that the normal teacher, as opposed to the 'abnormal' that would follow on, would be there to start the lesson off. This turned out to be the case, and the young, slim, PE teacher took the girls through an excruciating warm up exercise that included lifting the bottom skywards, feasible for the pert derriere but a gravitational impossibility for the more upholstered backside. She then handed me a piercing whistle, without any sort of disinfectant (I've never considered people who roll about in mud for a living microbiologically savvy; as a collective they simply don't care what they put in their mouths), instigated a loud pulsating drone from a CD player and told me to blow the whistle every sixty seconds. This was so that the girls, working in pairs, could take it in turns on a circus of equipment, including rowing machine, treadmill, exercise bike and weight machines. Nothing to it! Nothing it transpires other than a raging sore throat and thumping headache. The loud pulsating drone hit the torture button all by itself, without the need for the whistle, reverberating and ricocheting around the skull sixty times, to compound the pain. But as ever, I got little thanks for watching the clock so assiduously and heard one of the girls comment, 'That Mrs James gets paid money for old rope. She just sits on her bill and toots a whistle all day'. Little does the girl know how long it takes to practise the perfect blowing technique for shattering the glass of the fire alarm, but nil desperandum, I will keep on trying, I promise!

Yours truly

Beth

Treading on Eggshells

25.02.19

Dear Cassie,

I am convinced that I am going down with an eye infection, another biohazard of teaching, though one not necessarily linked to the whistle.

I have had the misfortune to come across a new pupil, Anthony, on the school exchange programme – expulsion, not French – one badass for another. The badass needs to have his name pronounced very specifically, An-th-ony, with emphasis on the 'th', to avoid his demonstration of the correct enunciation and spittle in the eye. I could have done with a shower cap, in fact any sort of cap, even one kicking about at the side of a vagina would have come in handy.

There has been a lot of tugging of the food technology apron strings recently. Any academic foolish enough to believe that boys and girls are the same, and any differences are only down to stereotypical upbringings, needs to examine the apron strings.

Girls easily tie a neat looping bow behind their backs; boys breathe in, truss themselves up in front fastening corset fashion, with a knot so tight Houdini would be challenged.

The reason I bring this to your attention is that it has been Civil War Day at school, with the pupils sporting pea shooters, compasses, sharpener blades, window poles and highlighter pens under closer scrutiny than normal. This is in a bid to make the miscreants sit still and watch attentively, primarily to reduce the feared external witness statement (what goes on in school stays in school).

The Civil War re- enactment, run by professionals, not the usual suspects, was brought to life with displays, period costume, talks, food of the time, muskets, pikes, and cannon fire.

From one of the talks – every day is a relentless school day – I gleaned that even the poor old Roundheads and Cavaliers couldn't get away from the condom lesson and sexual disease was rife at the time. Condoms were made from linen, or for the very well-endowed silk – less friction burn I suppose for those in the throes of trigonometry. However, the truly worrying aspect of the talk was that the condoms had to be secured in place by ribbons. After experiencing the boys' efforts in food technology, all I can say is that I wouldn't want to be the one charged with getting the circulation going on that score, and I sincerely hope that in the Roundhead and Cavalier manual of sixteen steps to tying on a condom, have a pair of manicure scissors at 'the side' (seems to be the favoured option of the moment) is top of the list.

At least the Roundheads and Cavaliers weren't burdened with having to make Scotch eggs, my latest food technology nightmare, and an assault on all five senses. I repeat all five, from the sulphurous odour, alopecia look, rubbery feel, volleys from the oven – yes the little buggers explode voluntarily without the need for cannon – to the taste, which I can't actually comment upon as I wouldn't touch one with a pike pole. Of all the dire food technology products to be scoffed at, not scoffed, the Scotch Egg wins the award. A deep-fried 'full English in a ball' although due to the inherent dangers of the fryers, the rubber balls were oven cooked, not daringly deep-fried.

The Scotch egg forms part of the Year 9 syllabus looking at portable foods with an edible casing, partial edibility being a more realistic criteria to meet than full edibility, but it's always better to run before you can jump. (One of my mother's stock seven, sayings that is, not the standard meals.)

The chop and grate at home rule was substituted (a refreshing change for parents' finger health) with 'hard boil' four eggs. Not quite the same as place an egg between two switched on mobile phones, that one girl reliably informed me her uncle had done, to get a thoroughly cooked egg in an eight-hour time period. I think I am vindicated in my mistrust of the mobile phone.

Anyway, the instruction to 'hard boil', not 'have a chat with', was to ease both lesson time constraints and egg transportation from home.

Foolishly, I thought that this would leave plenty of lesson time for the rest of the exercise, but I could have made a soufflé and got a Roundhead out of a tight predicament quicker than it took the pupils to shell a hardboiled egg.

The girls, under the impression they had a Faberge, delicately removed tiny fragments of shell that the Romans would have been grateful for, whilst the boys went for the juggling freestyle method of shell removal. I thought that one boy had gone down with mumps but if you can't juggle there are always other party tricks to fall back upon.

True skill, however, is being able to release sausage meat from a plastic tube that needs slicing at its tip. Blunt as ever, the school knives that is, I gave the command: 'A firm grip and a good squeeze should do the trick.'

I'm very cross-curricular these days but the girls lacked the requisite knack. Those looking green didn't fare much better despite the option of vegetarian sausage meat, but the pioneering Y sharing chromosome jugglers soon had sausage meat sticking to the fingers like shit to a shoe. I mean, the bloody stuff just doesn't come off, and it's no-good rubbing it with an egg because as I have now discovered, too late in the proceedings may I say, eggs come with their own Teflon coating.

Three hundred grams of sausage meat should have been quartered and moulded around each blackened, bruised specimen (when did the 'run a boiled egg under cold water' rule die out?) but eggs kept popping out of hands like ping pong balls fired from a fanny. (I know, I apologise, it is a Peter Kay 'Phoenix Night's' image I have never quite been able to come to terms with. Not the kind of act we want to replicate in the Christmas variety show with a red-faced Racing Billy hanging his head in shame in his Santa hat.) And it wasn't a good look for the non-listener trying to cloak four eggs with only seventy-five grams of sausage meat (my fault of course), when those working with three hundred grams had bald spots.

In between patching up and dealing with the nauseous and the fainting – honestly, I've grounds to sue with the state of my rotator cuff – came the 'roll your balls in breadcrumbs' challenge. Don't worry; it is never going to catch on to a bucket list for the skies. You are reprieved.

Firstly, the pupils had to coat their offerings with beaten egg, provided by the school, not the home – a sensible risk assessment minimising the possibility of the school being egged. Then the balls had to be dropped into a bag of breadcrumbs, shop bought or homemade, any preference but school made, and gently rolled around so that the breadcrumbs would stick to the egg washed sausage meat encasing the internal stink bomb.

I won't go into detail, as I presume you are in heaven and not hell, but try to envisage what happens when the Y chromosome gets the urge to shake the bag like maracas. Positively apocalyptic to lure a caretaker out of his lair, although, in an aggrieved tone, he said that the head had sent him to trace the origin of a pervasive smell permeating the school, not a mop job. I didn't care for his tone, very matter of fact and all knowing – 'Oh it's your doing, is it?' – as if essence of hydrogen sulphide was my daily choice of allure.

Next came a lightning bolt moment – not sausage meat deliberately or accidently poked into the electric sockets; the cloth never left my hand – but the true meaning behind the saying 'oh crumbs'. The industrially manufactured, standardised powder business that you operated in is a far cry from the 'crumb', a non-standardised SI unit ranging from millet to the full loaf.

Mr Seventy-Five Grams, fervently waving two slices of thick white, not breadcrumbs, under my nose needed to fall back on his excellent rubber shredding technique (erasers not condoms). I couldn't provide the help he was looking for because the classroom nut job demanded all my attention, and as per usual I hadn't been given the appropriate training. The task was to produce 'Scotch eggs', not multigrain fat balls for the garden bird feeder, prompting Mrs Prendergast to feverishly start printing and handing out storage instruction labels, to be passed on to the parents – 'Keep out of reach of the budgie.'

Fat balls, as it so happens, are also proving a divisive issue on the home front. After admiring some delightful tits in my garden, my mother, upon my advice (I should have known better – really, if daring to suggest downlights for the modern looking kitchen ceiling, as opposed to not one, but three extra length fluorescent lighting tubes, requiring the electricity generating capacity of their own nuclear reactor, hasn't taught me anything, then nothing will) decided to invest in some fat balls of her own, properly manufactured, not homemade. Proof of purchase will be catalogued in the ledgers. But rather than enticing little tits, with manners and a dainty nibble, what should swoop down but a damned big crow with the temerity to open its gob (another childhood banned word along with fanny that I have now worked up the courage to put on paper, heart rate difficult to control) and fly off with the fat ball whole. This is now my fault because I did not give the relevant danger warnings associated with the fat ball (in the case of the homemade variety enough roughage and fibre for a crow to rival the seagull shitting machine), and the experience has not provided my mother with value for money.

How was I supposed to know that there is a breed of crow that takes its dining advice from the cruise ship restaurant? Well, there's no danger of any child's family putting a rattling Scotch egg whole into the 'gob' for tonight's tea, with or without the necessary danger warnings or bedazzling illuminations; the rubber bullets can speak entirely for themselves.

Yours truly

Beth

Beyond the Pale

08.03.19

Dear Cassie,

By all accounts, the February half term ski trip has been a success, some figures holding up with no decline in patient numbers reported. Injuries listed so far (different children taking the strain): two sprained ankles, one broken leg, a bust lip, chin in need of butterfly stitches, dislocated shoulder, brace no longer fitting and a lost cap (from the tooth, not the head or a darker, more furtive place).

I haven't been on a school trip since 1986. The trip was a weekly outing, to be precise, carried out over the spring term, to visit a woodland setting; one situated approximately thirty yards from school. The aim of the weekly jaunt was to study the nature of trees, from bark to sticky buds, to galling leaves (a swelling caused by insects, fungi, bacteria, or external damage), as part of a GCSE biology woodland project. The first year of study, as it happens, for the new GCSE course designed to replace 'O'level in 1988 and in its infancy. The only trouble with the woodland setting is that there are more hiding places than bears for pupils trying the limits of the inexperienced young teacher. That's not to say that the woodland project didn't have its merits. When it came to signing up for future school trips, how to remain successfully hidden in the woods, camouflaged under a pile of gall damaged leaves was invaluable.

Some people, on the other hand, never learn a valuable lesson. The PC has returned to the car wash and this time ruthlessly accused the rollers of taking away her actual body work, in the form of flakes of paint. Her father advised that if she had used a 'shammy' as previously instructed, this wouldn't have happened, but the PC replied that she didn't know what a 'shammy' was, let alone where to get one (a sad indictment on the state of modern-day policing).

Ever the teacher, wishing to expand hearts and minds, I patiently explained that 'shammy', was an abbreviation of Chamois, a type of leather, gentle but highly effective on cleaning body parts. But I'd obviously missed the point because rather than appropriate cleaning tactics, the PC was using flaky paint as code for 'I need a new car'.

'And where do you think you are going to get the money for that, bearing in mind that you have just got your first home?' I countered; but ask a silly question. It's all very well, but how many Scotch eggs does it take to pay for a Volkswagen Fox, even one five years of age with enough mileage under the belt for it to naturally know to steer clear of the rollers.

If flaking paint doesn't do the trick ('if at first you don't succeed, try, try again' really should be limited to educational attainment only), there is always the safety aspect, specifically broached in terms to engender parental fear, to fall back upon. 'You do want me to be safe, don't you?' in the no holds barred approach, 'and a Foxie would be so much safer than a thirteen-year-old Ka in holes'.

Keep out of the holes then – I thought that was the whole point of police driver training – and follow the family rule that cars, like Marks and Sparks pyjamas, are never swapped before they are, at the very least, fifteen years old – for the adult man, that is, not necessarily the growing child.

Needless to say, my advice was disregarded and without even a couple of weeks of persistent wheedling (all this assertiveness training can be taken too far), we were asked to attend a test drive of a Fox at the Car People, Warrington on Saturday afternoon, with only three hours' prior notice. I'm not sure which is the more shocking: being asked to cross the border, or thinking that we are available at three hours' notice, including travelling time, with no plans of our own for a depressingly wet weekend.

Well, upon arrival, I didn't need to get in it to see that it was white – not the best colour choice for those without the chamois. Clever marketing doesn't rest solely on the snuggle; there are some who genuinely believe that 'polar' won't show up so much as a speck in the light.

As for the interior design, I can't comment on the probability (one of the most difficult and disliked mathematical topics) of dashboard slide because I never got to see the angle of slope. Shouting out, apparently, is not 'de rigueur' on a test drive and so I was banned and dumped at the coffee machine to nurse a free drink that thirty minutes later ranked as the most expensive free beverage in history. Some people clearly think that I've got Scotch eggs to burn.

Pity that quiche, another Year 9 task fulfilling the edible casing criteria, doesn't burn, or even cook partly through, in the latest round of treading on eggshells with Mrs Prendergast. What Mrs P doesn't appreciate is that I have to mark the evaluations on 'food products with an edible casing' and 'flan' needs a lot less correction than 'quesh'.

The inherent problem with quiche cookery is that the edible casing only encases half of the product, leaving the other half on display. A thin skimming over is not full coagulation, but there are only so many times I can give the order, 'if it ripples, put it back'.

I should have used the wasted thirty minutes, sat idly (God forbid) at a coffee machine, to mark the various food product evaluations, including the infamous Scotch eggs, but now I have got the evaluations in front of me sloth comes highly recommended. Sometimes the pain is simply too great.

Q. How will this practical help you in the future?

A. It will help me when I am hungry.

(We have some very astute pupils.)

Q. If you were to carry out this practical again what would you do differently?

A. I wouldn't eat my Scotch eggs over Miss Lack's desk because she went mental over the grease stains.

(I've heard on the grapevine that Marlene isn't too happy over the state of the minibus either, but the first rule of defence is never to admit liability.)

Q. If you were to carry out this practical again, what would you do differently?

A. I wouldn't sit by Fred Turner because he put his washing

up in with mine for me to do.

Q. How could you improve the fibre content of your product?

A. Miss said that the fibre content of my Scotch egg was the most impressive she had seen and didn't need improvement.

Q. How would you describe your overall product?

A. Holesome and dilishus.

Well, I don't suppose I can argue with holesome and dilishus – I need appreciation from somewhere – but it does beg the question, 'what exactly are some children getting served up for tea?'.

Talking of appreciative meals, I was delighted when the PC asked, 'What are you doing on Mother's Day?' Here it comes, I thought, at long, long last, the Mother's Day invitation that my own mother has had for the last thirty-three consecutive years, without even waiting for the actual invite. 'You will be having us on Mother's Day, won't you?' more with menace than polite confirmation.

Right, I thought to myself, things are about to change: helping with a new home and a new Foxie, in lovely shade, has finally got its compensations. I didn't demur, 'never look a gift horse in the mouth' is not lost on me, and so confirmed that I would be available on Mother's Day for the Epicurean meal. 'Oh good,' was the response, 'because I always enjoy your Sunday roast on Mother's Day, you always make an extra effort when Gran and Granddad come for tea.'

At least my daughter enjoys my roast dinner without expressing the untold disappointment one young man had in PSE, after salivating at the thought of a BLT. This is the trouble when everything in life is reduced to acronyms, and the pupil mistakes a bacon, lettuce and tomato sandwich for the breasts, lumps, and testicles lesson. You want to try feeling your way round that lesson at short notice – practice makes perfect – although mercifully, prostheses are provided to demonstrate how to carry out self-examination and detect the early stages of cancer. I'll probably have to thank the girls a thousand times for touching a testicle, although the boys will need no gratitude with the knitted breasts.

It seems to me that teaching has become taken over by the thank you culture, in a system where pleading and thanking, working in tandem, are used all too frequently to achieve what should be the natural high expectation and outcome. Lining up sensibly, sitting down quietly, owning a pen and mastering it, the correct disposal of illegal chewing gum, the ability to draw a straight line under a title (I blame Olga – the flexible, bendable, functionless ruler that manufacturers can't even get a caning over)... do I need to go on? Well, yes, I do. Copying down the date, when supplied on the board for gratis, should, with intense training, not beseeching and eternal gratitude, be as natural as purchasing the home on the hill.

Don't misunderstand me, I'm wholeheartedly for good manners and politeness, but can't quite bring myself to say, 'thank you for being wonderful human beings'. (Some form tutors go over the top.) The sickliest I can aspire to is thank you most sincerely, kindly, warmly, humbly, gratefully, for hiding the evidence before Mrs Prendergast gets back!

Your own form members (lunchtime wolfing habits

nothing less than remarkable) don't need thanking for their Homo sapiens status, not when there are large art room tables with extra length oilcloths to kick and hide the remnants of the lunchtime buffet under. No need to get down on bended knee there!

Some years ago, as it so happens, I became quite proficient at the finger buffet, Scotch eggs excepting, courtesy of ten long weeks (double lessons doubling the pain) devoted to sandwiching making in GCSE food technology. I could have had sex (the lesson) and packed a family picnic, including a few spares for the bears, in less than ten minutes, not twenty long hours set aside for the chore. Most practical food technology lessons run desperately short of time, but with sarnies less likely to ride up the arm, sandwich-making proved the exception to the rule.

All manner of tactics were employed to pan out the sandwiches but as a master of panning (the supply teacher's overriding skill), even I couldn't get a handle on the problem. I mean, there is panning and there is panning.

The target audience was a fundamental feature, with great thought given to the sandwich consumer. The brief was for a businessman – pristine suit, shirt, and tie – so the overstuffed sandwich with exploding filling had to be avoided at all costs, the dry cleaning included.

The pupils, especially the boys, couldn't get past the notion that they would be the ones eating the sandwich, not the businessman, and so en masse, inspirationally came up with the bacon butty with tomato ketchup for the businessman heavily invested in haulage.

The girls in the class, less interested in tachometers, provided the little extra refinements and details (not the handprint) that the boys' sandwiches were so sadly lacking. An impressive prawn salad on granary, with the lettuce so washed it provided the natural environment for the prawn. And as for the businessman in need of tightening the tubbier trucker's belt, there is always the magic of the Dairylea triangle, spread parsimoniously over two bone-dry Ryvitas, to hold out a morsel of hope!

Yours truly

Beth

The Proof is in the Pudding

20.03.19

Dear Cassie,

Any family members thinking that they are going to finish off with blackberry and apple crumble on Mother's Day, in twelve months' time, are going to be sadly disappointed. I never want to see another fruit crumble for as long as I live, and would prefer to earn my living demonstrating, daily, the 'glow in the dark' condom. Try getting a flicker out of one of those buggers and you'll be lucky. The collective classroom disappointment, falling solely on my shoulders, was on a par to not providing the bacon butties.

Fruit crumbles are a Year 8 task with two intrinsic dangers – although thankfully not electrocution as a last resort – the fruit, and the crumble.

The fruit, surprisingly, had to be prepared in school, to develop peeling and slicing skills, and moreover to give a brief respite for parents accustomed to working their fingers to the bone.

I demonstrated how to peel, quarter, and core an apple but Mrs P was quick to point out that my claw grip technique for slicing the fruit was inadequate. We don't all share her advantage.

Mistakenly hearing a tin of sliced peaches for two large cooking apples (I suppose we have all been there) did confer an advantage over the blood/protein element to the dish for one pupil who found the claw grip for opening the can very cutting. How to use a can opener safely must take precedence on how to reduce the school lighting bill, as a matter of public priority, for the next governors' meeting.

The crumble element also had to be made in school, so that any advanced sightings of a multi nutty grain loaf could be removed at source for those that misheard bird seed crumbs for crumble.

For the crumble making process itself, a scatter gun firing crumbs at velocity could not have bettered the efforts of the rubbing in fingertip approach. If only I could get them to stop rubbing their fingertips in the cutlery drawer, along the work surfaces, window ledges, taps, ovens and hobs, the food room wouldn't look like the aftermath of a powerful dust storm.

A small part of the flour element used in the recipe had to be replaced with fibre, such as crushed Weetabix, or rolled oats, to make the crumble mix into a healthy, high fibre topping. This gave the toppings a vastly different look, ranging from the perfect way to start the day the Scottish way, to the lining of a guinea pig's cage. So, you can imagine the immense sense of relief when I read one boy's answer to the evaluation question 'How did your product turn out?'.

'My product turned out like apple crumble. If you had to buy it, you would say that is an apple crumble.'

Hallelujah, praise be to the Lord, my prayers have finally

been answered! What pure unadulterated joy.

Other evaluation question and answers included:

Q. Did you have any difficulties in your practical work and how did you overcome them?

A. I had difficulty peeling the apples for my apple crumble and so I gave them to my friend to peel. (I'll make a note to put forward for the gifted and talented.)

Q. How could you improve the taste and flavour of your product?

A. I could add desecrated coconut to the topping.

Q. What did you think about your choice of filling?

A. In my opinion, my filling was a good choice because I chose one that I knew all my family would eat (my brother is a fussy eater). My mum insisted that I use rudard but I said no because we have all got to be able to eat it.

Q. What did your family think to the product?

A. Personally I believe that my apple crumble turned out well as my family (plus guest) enjoyed it as a pudding with custard. The guest comes for his tea every Tuesday which is a nuisance.

A. My fruit crumble was a great success in my house; everybody including me thought it was delicious. My Grandma said that the topping was beautifully light and better than she could have made. She thinks I have a real touch and the crumble was as good as my last week's light as a feather scones.

Q. What have you learnt from this practical?

A. Not to put it in my bag sideways.

A. To wear oven gloves when lifting out of the oven.

Q. How would you describe your overall product?

A. A heavenly match of fruit to topping.

I know what you are thinking because truth to tell I am thinking the same thing, who was the guest treated to fruit crumble as an actual pudding, not the breakfast option, and was it a VIP guest – there's obviously been some ceremony attached with the laying on of custard. Anyway, I've made a mental note to do some quizzing and investigative work and will let you know in my next correspondence.

In the latest news on the home front, the lodger has finally come in handy. He answered the telephone ringing at ten o'clock at night, a serious breach of telephone etiquette, before it disturbed our sleep. The offender, despite the eight o'clock at the latest rule, was none other than the PC herself, with a report of water coming in through the bedroom ceiling. There seems to be some misunderstanding as to which family members make up the emergency services when Alexa can't come up with a mop and bucket.

Fortunately, the call handler wasn't prepared to put the call through to us unless the caller, still breathing, was prepared to take full responsibility for a rude awakening and so news didn't reach us until the following morning. Expecting your parents to fling themselves across a roof top in the dark, to stop Gareth getting in – the storm, not the man, but we live in hope – is a bit much, don't you think, although growing up I never expected to be on first name terms with a storm. It's a poor friend that wilfully knocks your garden pots over, tipples neighbours' rubbish onto the drive and then beggars off with the shed roof felt tucked under his arm.

To de-stress (it's not just the aftereffects of the storm; I have been dragooned into teaching drama again – the only subject to make sociology look structured), I thought that I would start the PC's garden efforts off; after all she has to start somewhere. So, I began with a pair of beautifully planted up, by my own hand and at some cost, upright (no thanks to Gareth), large, aquamarine glazed terracotta pots that I coveted for my own garden. However, the PC's face hit the ground faster than when stood in the spotlight as she eyed the floral beauties.

'Appreciate' would be the answer to the question, 'What do you expect me to do with those?'. Start with tending a Hebe and you never know, nurturing a baby may be next. Hence, with increased purpose and resolve I managed 'I expect you to put them in the courtyard' (technically it's a yard shared with three other houses but there's no need to let my sister and sister-in-law know, three hundred miles further south and it would be a mews), pointing out, 'Somebody needs to lead the way in the living garden pot, as opposed to the deceased kind, decorated with spinning windmills, fairies on sticks, strings of shiny beads and bare arsed gnomes'. With such tasteless vulgarity I don't expect Monty and his crew will be knocking round to the mews any time soon.

Thus, as I was artfully arranging 'decorum in a container' for those with RHS membership, one of the PC's neighbours came out to say hello.

In addition to the normal pleasantries and introductions, I thought she had come out to admire my handiwork, but instead of basking in a warm glow of praise I was subjected to the 'nail it down' lecture. 'Everything round here,' apparently, 'has to be 'nailed down',' or, and I quote, 'the thieving little bastards will have it. They've already been in yours, twice as it happens, front and back. (Painful.) They'll take anything they can get their thieving hands on, so nail the bloody lot'.

At this litany I began to empathise with the tongue tied, self-conscious, excruciatingly reticent and reserved drama pupil, devoid even of the 'costume is in the wash excuse' for nonparticipation. (It's only the grand theatrical performances that require the services of Honeypots as a dresser, not the actual lessons.) I simply had no words or any idea how to react to such distressing neighbourly news other than wait until I get my hands on the mendacious estate agent. If drama has taught me anything, it is always that violence is the answer. Without fail, every single drama group performance ends in a mass brawl and any subject dependent on the raucous, clamorous fracas for developing skills needs to be consigned to the 'of no use whatsoever' box, along with over eager estate agent, economical with the truth.

So, considering the updated crime figures, you can imagine my concern for the glazed terracottas when my own mother had looked as if she could whip them out from under my very nose. My mother is a passionate gardener and deeply knowledgeable plants woman with a wonderful garden of her own, and she knows a good thing when she sees it. (My dad, apparently, at the age of five, in the infant school playground – we are a family who know how to stay the course.)

When I finally found my voice (loud and clear, head held high, no sniggering, smirking, sniffing –whatever happened to the handkerchief – shuffling, swaying, swaggering – there are some overly dramatic types, or tomfoolery) and looked the crime statistician directly in the eye, I announced 'I don't think I can actually nail down a pot; it's probably best if I just take the pair back home with me,' secretly thrilled.

'Oh, you don't need to worry over those, love, the little bastards won't touch them. They're only after what they can sell.'

There's no accounting for taste, as the school cookery evaluation clearly demonstrates, but on the select side of the Alps, an up-market terracotta pot, with plants biochemically photosynthesising and respiring, would sell only too well.

Yours truly

Beth

Passing the Buck

17.04.19

Dear Cassie,

Well, the Upper Mill roofer, found via the Upper Mill Facebook group – not a method I would choose; I don't want to be drawn into any sort of cult – has been summoned and given his expert advice that if you can see daylight when you lift the loft hatch, there is a hole.

No shit, Sherlock. Apologies, it's the English department's alliterative message finally getting through, or it was for the pupil's example of my dad likes a s..., shower and shave. Three guesses will not be needed for whether that was a male, female, or gender fluid pupil's alliterative example.

We are now waiting for the quote, but I do not the like the game of my daughter went to market and bought a snuggle, log burner, log store (any chance of some logs?), Foxie – five years old, sixty-six thousand miles on the clock – and now a potential new roof.

As the external log store looks out of bounds – 'You're not going to risk putting wood in that with the light fingered around here, are you?' – I'm thinking that chopping the log store up might be the answer to the shortage of actual logs and bringing the job lot inside. Unless, of course, the thieving little bastards, in addition to getting into 'yours', via the front and back passage, are going to go for the directly overhead approach and swing on down from on high. I despair. A few months is all it has taken before major repairs.

The installation of the log burner – our gift to the PC and not part of the credit loans – has also had issues. As ever, I was solely on hand to oversee operations, when one of the two fitters said, 'Where do you want it, love, front or back?' I'm not kidding, it's the latest craze.

I replied, 'I think the chimney breast would be best.' It does make you wonder about the state of the Lancashire schools, but he was referring to the rubble created from the opening of the chimney breast and seemed to think that I was in some way mentally defective for not knowing, in advance, that we should have ordered a skip. Once I fully understood the nature of the problem, I responded, 'Oh, the back, definitely' – there's no chance of having to incur skip costs when, with a little bit of help, the bricks will be able to remove themselves.

I am under strict instructions to keep the PC's occupation secret from the new neighbours in case they are uncomfortable with her feeling their collars. I commented, 'Forget what they are wearing, don't you think they will think it funny with you coming and going at all hours of the day?' But my sister-in-law, birthday Burns, with her usual charm and acerbic wit said, 'Oh, they'll just think it's the entertainer in and out.' By jingo, birthday celebrations held at the Rabbie Burns poetry appreciation society are looking up.

Anyhow, we have met the neighbour for a second time –
Paula, thirty something, one partner, two children, and baby,
baby, baby (a two-year-old tortoise, not triplets, by the name
of Gonzalez) – and this time she provided the reassuring
advice 'these houses are sinking, you know'. A fact generally
more useful to know before purchase than after, but hey ho,
and confirmed this by way of the fact 'I used to have a step'.
Can't think why she didn't follow her own advice and nail it
down before it disappeared with the rest of the goods being
filched by the 'wrong uns round here'.

Her next morsel of cheer was that the previous incumbent
of the PC's home had 'passed', although obviously not from
tripping. I had to bite my tongue not to sound like my mother
– 'with distinction, I trust?' I sat a lot of Royal School of Music
piano exams as a child. If pupils learned to correctly answer
the comprehension task in full sentences, it may help them
to achieve the full verbal sentence in adulthood. This would
give clarity as to whether a person had passed the butter, salt,
baton, parcel or driving test.

Following all the new neighbourly chit chat – 'the gutter
on yours has pulled on ours and now our down pipe leaks
like a drain' (yours and ours being shorthand for your house
and our house for those beyond comprehension) – it was
ironic that I should be given a RPSE lesson to teach, entitled
' What makes a good neighbour?' The head of RPSE, Miss
Lines (name not punishment meted), assured me that this
was a meaningful learning task, although I doubt there is
anyone left in the country that doesn't comprehend the value
of 'meaningful'.

The task was a discussion exercise, earmuffs at the ready, thereby reducing the chances of Big Mac being buried under a pile of incorrectly stacked written answers (shame).

The pupils had to read four statements and then discuss whether they agreed or disagreed with the statements.

1. A good neighbour is someone who keeps themselves to themselves.

2. A good neighbour is involved in the local community and helps other people out.

3. A good neighbour does not complain over loud music and parties.

4. A good neighbour will lend money out and not expect to be paid back.

The four choices whittled down to two if you assume, as I do, that statement four was a typing error for 'parent' and statement three carried too much teenage bias, don't begin to scratch the surface of discussion for neighbourly advice. The general nub of the lesson, treat unto others as you wish to be treated yourself, is all very well, but never miss a golden chance to get down to specifics. Consequently, I decided to come up with some statements of my own to play the, agree or disagree, game.

1. A good neighbour is someone who doesn't allow their Christmas tree to roll around the garden from Twelfth Night to Shrove Tuesday, waiting for Gareth to pick up the needles and drop a forest floor off next door. (There's nothing gets my goat more, especially when I'm one hundred percent (nothing less expected) artificial.)

2. A good neighbour is someone who keeps their free-range

flock under tight lock and key. (Put the strays in the trophy cabinet, not my garden.)

3. A good neighbour is someone who should have more sense than to use the humane mouse trap (throwing good money after bad.)

4. A good neighbour is someone who issues formal dress code to the garden gnome. (In geography, it's known as gentrification.)

5. A good neighbour understands the correct balance of moss to lawn and acquaints himself/herself with a lawnmower now and then. (Preferably every five days for the longer but frequent superior cut.)

6. An exceptional neighbour goes to night classes to learn about vegetation management and excels in a field of weeds. (I'll pay the subscription.)

I could go on, it's quite a stress reliever being able to put into words my everyday frustrations, but I would be writing to you into next week to cover the tip of the iceberg.

So, calming down and turning my attention to school matters, I have found out about the mystery guest being served apple crumble, astonishingly as a pudding, with custard.

The guest, described in the evaluation as a nuisance for his weekly appearance, was not a VIP or undercover food critic, sampling the delights of school cooking, but the male pupil's older sister's boyfriend. The irritation did not stem from having a reduced portion of pudding with custard – some families (a tiny minority – oddities) know how to share amicably – but from the fact that too much kissing and hand holding had been going on at the tea table. If the weekly school tea isn't a test of true love, I don't know what is.

Marlene has started issuing her own MOTs (mess on the seats) for the school minibuses, following, allegedly, the deconstruction of a Scotch egg.

There has only been one false fire alarm this week. The science department has got messaging from a burning splint, worthy of the Navajos, down to a fine art, in the rigorous testing of the hypothesis 'there is no smoke without fire'.

There is to be a crackdown on pupils arriving late to morning registration and lessons, and a serious investigation into the reasons for the tardiness. The council has teenage torpor summed up in one, with the new sign placed outside the school gates: 'SLOW children crossing'. A remarkably astute observation by a council clearly cognisant with the fact the adolescence is not naturally programmed for 'move it'. However, in all fairness, the school buses don't always help the situation, one bus running so late that the driver could only sum it up as a flask and sandwiches job.

The recycling message (use common sense, magic fairies not available) continues to go round and round, sustainably, with more tedium and regularity than 'get to lessons on time'. The correct disposal of water bottles – 'I'm sorry, Miss, I'll never throw it again' – and paper aeroplanes – 'I'm sorry, Miss, I didn't know you wanted us to actually write something in the debate' (always – it's quieter) – is one thing, but the DIY burial of a Dalmatian dog, our neighbour's cost cutting efforts to avoid pet crematorium fees, entirely another. That really is taking recycling and the study of natural cycles (carbon and nitrogen) and the process of decomposition to a whole new level. For goodness sakes, don't tell Big Mac, or he will be hiring out the school playing fields.

However, the moral of the story, a good one for the next RPSE lesson delivered at two minutes' notice, is be careful what you wish for, as digging a garden over, special attention to the ill-kempt borders, is not the same as dig a bloody great hole, in the middle of the lawn, to put poor old Dexter, dead as a dodo, Dalmatian in.

In conclusion, if you really are desperate to get a heavenly neighbour certificate in assembly, there's nothing that exercises the resource ladies more than certificate production – 'don't do a moony on the minibus, replant your Christmas tree, fir or fibre optic, keep pets with a pulse under control, bury those that don't within the boundary of the title deeds, or alternatively, if thinking of cremation, Bryant and May only, no wooden splints nicked from science, and certainly not when your neighbour's washing is hanging out. Compost and recycle, anything and everything, all pets included and by following these guidelines you should find yourself duly rewarded!

Yours truly

Beth

The Milk of Human Kindness

14.05.19

Dear Cassie,

I hope that under the circumstances I didn't upset you with my last letter on Dexter the Dalmatian's crude disposal. I didn't mean to be insensitive, but when you were ill, you stressed many, many times, to carry on as normal and make no allowance for your situation, which is fortuitous as I have more to share on the subject.

My brother-in-law, the power station king, supported the DIY approach tightly afforded Dexter by my neighbours, on the grounds (even their own) that burial is greener for the environment. I replied that normal people rely upon 'A Cut above the Rest' to green up the lawn, with specialist NPK fertiliser, not a spot of Dalmatian.

However, the Power Station Quarterly must be a more exciting read than previously given credit for, worthy of at least a cursory flick, because my brother-in-law's view has been influenced by the deteriorating air quality around crematoria, due to the amalgam filling putting too much mercury into the atmosphere. He's quite obsessive about air quality and it makes you wonder what he's stoking the power station with. The point is though – and I thought I made a particularly good point, for one of less academic rigour – how many Dalmatians with dodgy dentition have you seen sitting back and relaxing in the dentist's chair?

Sitting in the dentist chair for a root canal, praying that effective sterilisation between patients is being upheld, would be less stressful than this week's daily diet of distress. Lateness has been left behind in favour of a new initiative drive on homework. The 'drive' being as good a place to leave it as the car, bus, minibus, bus stop, bedroom, school bag (I know it's in there somewhere), school bag on the roof (I've nearly reached it), school bag gone for a swim (I can explain why I am not in uniform), Mum's house, Dad's house, possibly Gran's house, changing rooms, locker, lunch hall and Fuengirola.

What was wrong with the good old-fashioned approach of 'Dexter did it'? Now I must endure the social media fetish for the minute-by-minute sob story, 'it's still drying out', without giving the homework transgressor something to really sob about. Not everyone shares your school of homework thought, with gummy bears and the kindly 'don't go worrying about it, love, bring it in tomorrow'. A deadline is a deadline, no excuses given, and pupils should fall on their swords, not the garden fork, when the deadline is broken.

'Well, Miss, it was like this. I was playing out last night, jumped off the garden wall and got impaled on the garden fork, so I had to go to Casualty. My dad took me, but my mum wasn't very pleased because he was in the middle of painting the kitchen buttercup yellow and the mess is getting on her nerves. We were there ages because Casualty had stopped serving and by the time we got back the brush had gone hard.'

'Really, Thomas, Casualty stopped serving?' Such ramblings are enough to have me reaching for the sweetie jar, if only for the gobstopper to take over from where the fork failed to pierce the tongue. I haven't time for this when the quiches are thinking of floating themselves home. Even when you think the terminally boring excuse has reached a conclusion it continues. 'Yes, Miss, they had to stop serving because a woman came in who was right bad, that bad she couldn't breathe and so she got right to the front of the queue. I can show you the dressing if you would like, it got me right here, under the rib.'

'Only if it is blue.' I wouldn't want Mrs P accusing me of breaking health and safety laws for not having the appropriate dressing for the salad to accompany the quiche.

The numerous parental letters arising from homework issues continue unabated.

Dear Mrs James,

Alasdair has not done his food technology homework because he has lost his folder. It is most unusual for Alasdair to lose a school item as he keeps all his books and folders in one place at home. He wonders if someone else took his folder as you have him very squashed up and there is no room where he is sitting.

Dear Mrs James

Kirsty has done her homework, but her Dad was involved

in a crash last night and the car was 'wrote off'. Her homework was in the car and now it has gone with the 'wrote off' car. The same thing happened to her reading book; can she borrow one so that Mr Mutters won't shout at her?

Dear Mrs James,

Toby had noted in his planner that homework was due in on Friday 22nd, not Friday 15th. This was a genuine error. However, even if the deadline had been the 22nd, Toby could not have done his homework because he needed a school computer as the home computer has gone for repair and the school computer rooms are either shut or full of people queuing at lunch time. Your comment regarding 'it's a hard life,' is true, especially when I tried to ring you at 1550 hours, and you had already gone. I will tell Toby not to eat in future at lunchtime, so that he can queue up for an hour to use a computer to do your homework.

Dear Mrs James,

I think it is ridiculous that 'X' has been given fifty lines for not having his planner signed by a parent. He did ask me, but I forgot. He has not done this before, and I think some modicum of common sense should prevail. 'X' has a life outside of school and he is busy every weeknight. The completion of these lines has meant less time spent on homework. If only you were more vigilant regarding the disgusting incident of the chewing gum ruining his trousers.

Squashing, starving, and sticking the little blighters to the spot is rather good going for one week's work, wouldn't you say?! Bring it on.

It should be remembered, however, that letters of complaint are not all one-way traffic. When I was a full-time chemistry teacher, I remember that the head of science had to write home because a fifteen-year-old boy constantly disturbed her lesson by noisily and deliberately breaking wind. The boy was preposterously proud and amused by his achievements. The mother wrote back to apologise for her son's flatulence, but with the addendum, 'like father like son'. It's always wise to know who to steer clear of at Parents' Evening.

I might be struggling to lift a hefty mail bag, but I don't need the services of a crane. A search and rescue operation is underway to locate 'Eloise of Lourdes', last seen two days ago. A mountain of incompetently stacked stray PE kits, sent her way for redistribution, is thought to be the reason behind the disappearance. Big Mac is digging with his bare hands (a speciality) as I write. Well, he better get to her soon because we have a mother on the warpath and there is no species more dangerous than a mother roused to ire, banging her fists on the headteacher's door. 'Mum' is riled because she believes that her daughter's missing gym kit may have been 'stolen' (shock horror) rather than misplaced. 'Stolen, madam, oh no, not in this school.' That is if the headteacher is reading from the appropriate cue card and hasn't mistakenly picked up 'Bullying, madam, oh no, not in this school'. It's to be hoped that 'Eloise of Lourdes' can come up with the goods quickly, as she surfaces for air, specifically, a blue gym bag, possibly navy. A gym bag that may or may not have the girl's name inside. A gym bag that may or may not have a full PE kit inside, possibly one or two items missing (let me guess, one Converse shoe, not two). A bag that may or may not have been left in room W7. However, there's no may or may not be about it: Mum is definitely not happy!

She's not the only one crying into her beer. Some of us are crying into our milk, a jug of milk, to be precise, with floating fly.

To cut down on the school corridor spillage trails, more from dairy than the placing of eggs all in one basket, or the ridiculously cavernous school bag, I decided to kindly provide the milk needed for the chocolate chip cookie baking exercise and charge pupils five pence each for the service. Ten pounds per head would not have been too much to ask for the calamity of that flawed decision; talk about in for a penny in for a pound.

The head of department, as in the genuine head of food technology, not plenipotentiary Prendergast in ambassadorial role, had helped herself to some of the milk in the fridge, especially assigned for the baking process, for her morning coffee, or three. In fact, I would go as far as saying the woman has a permanent milky moustache. Consequently, the milk quota was already short before the dirty bastard bluebottle did a kamikaze nosedive into the measuring jug that I was using to carefully pour out precise individual portions. Some days I really do feel that it is me against the world.

Not all pupils can be deflected with 'it's only a currant', and when I furtively tried dilution, to make up the missing fluid ounces, a sharp-eyed young Yorkshire man, forgetting his upbringing of hear all, see all, say nowt, shouted out, 'Hey Miss, what y'doing, I'm not stumping up for nowt but wata, we're not all on teachers wages tha knows.'

And don't I know it. How hard can it be to cough up a five pence piece when I haven't the wherewithal to give change for individual pound coins, leading to yet more hand wringing because as Mrs P so rightly pointed out, the germ riddled coins had exchanged hands after compulsory hand washing at the start of the lesson had been completed.

Scrubbing up for the exchange of coins, or the handwritten cheque, hairnet and apron at the ready, won't be necessary for much longer, when recipients of celebratory gifts such as birthdays and weddings think it acceptable to provide their direct bank account number. The present-day wedding invitation seems to follow the lines of 'We do not wish for any wedding gifts; your presence is far more important to us than any gifts. However (there it is, the ubiquitous however), if you would like to contribute to our honeymoon the bank account number is...'

No, I would not like to contribute to the maxi moon, the 'round a world' holiday of a lifetime taken three months after the wedding, as opposed to the immediate mini moon, to allow for the filling and counting of the bank account coffers. I had to be grateful for a peg bag at my wedding, an inspired gift, not featuring on the formal list, which needless to point out, came from Stuart's side.

Monetary value can be a moot point in the classroom. When pupils are asked to knuckle down and get on with their work, an all too frequent response is, 'Why should we when we're not getting paid for it?' However, when the tables are turned, more unruly behaviour, it is met with, 'You're getting paid for it, aren't you?' Well then, that's tickety-boo.

If it's not riches beyond compare, bringing out the green-eyed monster, it is the number of school holidays bestowed upon the teacher. I wish I could have a five pence piece, handled with kid gloves and a disinfectant spray gun, every time my neighbour labours, 'We could all do with your holidays.' The PC, rather more mercenary, says she wishes she could have a pound coin for every time the comment is made, 'You never catch em, do you?' So, I suppose, in the end, one way and another, all jobs have a cross to bear. To engender the public sympathy vote I think it best that we take up employment in the china department of John Lewis, presiding over a wedding present list (measuring jug to be recommended and most useful) that has long since had its day.

Yours truly

Beth

Taking the Biscuit

23.05.19

Dear Cassie,

I am thinking of you today, on what would have been your forty-seventh birthday, with a plentiful supply of Florentines to mark the occasion. Cherished memories of you will always be locked in my heart; the Florentines are under a different form of lock, one where I oversee the key. Rest assured there will be no one helping themselves on my watch; no need to worry on that score.

An-th-on-y, pass a handkerchief please, wouldn't give a fraction on the maths problem being asked of him. The question in the textbook stated that there are five sweets in a bag. Two of them are lemon flavoured and three of them are orange flavoured. What fraction of the sweets is orange flavoured?

Exasperatingly, half an hour later, I was still patiently and calmly trying to tease out the answer, acting skills masking all signs of being close to hitting the throttle button. I asked him again, in between deep breaths, to look again at the picture of the five sweets in the textbook, in their relevant colours. His only response was that the job had him licked, an unfortunate turn of phrase with prosecutions pending. However, An-th-on-y, rather astutely, was quite right to draw this conclusion. A teacher worth their salt knows when to concede defeat. The textbook did indeed show orange and lemon sweets, but the non-existent bag remained something of a mystery.

No quarter was given (fractions eschewed across the board) in food technology's taste testing exercise, the lesson of all lessons in taking the biscuit. The lesson objective here, to show pupils how food technologists in industry, developing new food products, taste the fruits of their labour, made the task of teaching fractions, with a paper bag over the head, look easy.

The pupils in the class were given a quarter each of five different branded biscuits and asked to rate them on a scale of one to five for crunchiness, sweetness, brownness, flavour, and mouth feel. The ratings were then visually displayed on a star diagram for analysis. Now, before we even get to the male of the species, capable of throwing a quarter of a biscuit to ceiling height and starting acid digestion as the quarter makes its way back down, without it so much as touching the sides, leaving the criteria of 'mouth feel' off the scale, there are lots of snags with this lesson. Twenty-five pupils, and one hundred and twenty-five quarters is an awful lot of careful cutting, counting, and dishing out, for those snatching the biscuit without any understanding of fractions and equal portions. The Chocolate Digestives were under, the Ginger Nuts (legitimate classroom name calling) over and the Shortbreads somewhere in between.

Each child, altruistically, was provided with a free glass of undiluted water (no need for the exchange of coins). This was to cleanse the palate between each taste testing session, not provide a medium to facilitate dunking. The principles of dissolving, solvents, solutes, solubility, and saturated solutions need to remain firmly the domain of science. And have you ever tried quartering biscuits with deadly flying fragments firing off in all directions? Moreover, who wants to think about brownness and mouth feel simultaneously, most unappetising. It has got to a pretty pass when the only way to get out of such a senseless lesson is to cry 'nut allergy', with the allergic reaction to the hamster cheeked pupil, not anaphylaxis from the peanut or the cashew.

The only type of biscuit not to feature on the taste testing list was the Custard Cream, yet it still managed to upset my day, for reasons which will become apparent.

At the PC's swearing in ceremony (school pupils and Mrs Braithwaite could give the police a run for their money on that one), we were expecting a slap up do. This was because previously, when Meg was a Special Constable and had to be sworn in, a feast was provided for attending parents upon conclusion of the ceremony.

A feast for the eyes, all things told, because as good citizens, taught never to push or shove, Stuart and I patiently waited in the buffet queue together, rather than having the wit for one of us to dash, grab and commandeer the nearest table. Quite a spectacle. Consequently, we had delicious looking food on a plate but nowhere to balance it.

Indeed, we were so slow off the mark that we didn't get

the opportunity to put into practice my mother's dining table rule of 'It is always polite to say no thank you to second helpings on the first time of asking but you may accept if they are offered a second time'. No need to worry, Mother, we couldn't manage to get the first helpings off the plate, let alone seconds and thirds, although some of the other parents had a bloody good go. I don't know if the police are recruiting on the grounds of 'it pays to know thy quarry' but not all the parents looked savoury and I don't care if there is a heatwave, the flip flop and polo shirt are no substitute for the suit, shirt and collar and the immaculately buffed court shoe. The natural gravitation to the 'casual', as opposed to the smart, simply goes to show the failings of the smart casual dress code.

So, wise to the event, when it came to the next ceremony (under no circumstances at this one, according to a most insistent Meg, to give a ranking score to every male recruit passing out, difficult when marking is in the blood) I remarked, 'I'll get the table, you source the food' (we are very up to date with the correct food parlance).

Well, believe you me; we hadn't saved ourselves, not even a biting on, for the hunter-gatherer to return with a miserly Custard Cream and cup of tea. I can testify, first-hand, that the police budget cuts are biting. I nearly bit into the table with hunger and disappointment; there are some noticeably short male police officers these days, with a less than adequate foot size for comparable purposes. Furthermore, breathing the same rarefied air as the Chief Con (that would be Chief Constable to you – I'm on friendlier terms having shared a cup of char) does not assuage the hunger pangs at Custard's last stand when you've got a rare appetite and rapidly dropping blood sugar levels. The biggest con in history to make us willingly give up our five o'clocks. Why, I could see from the chap's frame that he hadn't got to where he is today on Custard Creams alone, whether served crumbed, quartered or whole.

Exceedingly disappointing ceremonies aside (not an exceedingly good cake in sight), all part of life's rich tapestry, the only thing worse than trying to hang, draw and quarter a ginger biscuit is to bake the bugger in the first place.

Combining two skills in one lesson, melting (butter and treacle) and mixing dry ingredients (flour, ginger and sugar) into the melt doesn't do, far too challenging, especially when the plastic tray requisitioned for baking the biscuits on is not a baking tray at all, but the non-oven proof stand for the oil pot used for greasing the actual trays. Can you imagine Mrs P's dumbfounded disbelief and reaction to the toxic, choking fumes as the plastic melted and moulded itself over the insides of the oven with the ginger biscuit mixture, a viscous molten lava, sliding in slow motion, off the top? Every alarm bell and monitor in the food technology room gratingly ringing and pinging, with the fire engine expensively revving up.

The midst of a major, polluting industrial accident is not the best time for Mr Seventy-five grams to ask me what to do with his tin of Heinz Treacle Pudding. He's not going to be gaining any marks for this week's evaluation which presumably will be along the lines of:

Q. How did the ginger biscuits turn out?

A. My ginger biscuits turned out as a Heinz can of treacle pudding that my family, including sycophantic Grandma, were incredibly proud of. We shall be eating the treacle pudding as a pudding, with custard, and guest. (Cannibalism at its best.)

Q. What would you do differently if you were to do this practical again?

A. I would open my cloth ears and use treacle not treacle bloody pudding in the cooking process, apologies for the swearing but my limit of patience really is wearing thin.

And then, to add insult to injury I got a parent daring to question the department's teaching techniques.

Dear Mrs James,

We have enjoyed the food technology output, but I'm not convinced of the benefit of simply mixing ingredients together at school that have been prepared at home. Would you care to comment?

No, I would not care to comment. But if the parent is looking for output, the ginger biscuit experience is the way to go. I am not surprised the oil pot tray was requisitioned – the recipe churned out more biscuits than a Fox's factory and the baking trays were brimming within minutes. The rounds of dough melded together to form a solid rectangular granite mass, the mother of all ginger nuts. Hanging, drawing, and quartering is too good for some but there was little choice when the product needed to resemble baked goods destined for home transportation.

It won't just be Paddy, back from his transatlantic travels, nursing a cracked tooth, in the dentist's chair this week.

Away from the art of stone masonry, I have been devoting myself to office supplies; there's more than one way of making the arm ache. The Roundheads and Cavaliers weren't burdened with an aching writing arm because they couldn't afford a pen. A good quality quill was more expensive than a house. Honestly, I just soak it up like a sponge.

Nowadays, pens are plentiful and cheap, but for the school species 'nopendo' – 'I can't do it because I haven't got a pen' – still out of arm's reach. The clever and artful game of written work avoidance comes at a cost, especially for the one with the middle name W.H. Smiths trying to circumvent the problem. In doing so, I am breaking one of my mother's fundamental rules, 'never a borrower or lender be', so at the very least I expect the recipient of my kindness to politely return the writing implement at the end of the lesson, fully intact, not throw it, dismantle it, ping it, as in the spring, keep for the trophy chest or use it for a drink. Hands, lips, tongue, and teeth do not look good in blue or black, but it doesn't wash with me when the pupil demands, 'You will have to let me out to the toilets now'. I will not be blackmailed or give in to the threat, 'I'll get you done'. More confusion with the incomplete sentence, will that be done as in 'my grandma said that my keysh was done to a turn', or my experience that most things, other than the wishy-washy quiche, are done to a crisp?

One irascible young man arriving late to the lesson, and

failing to volunteer, as should be customary, a reason for his lateness, sat down and promptly proceeded to stare into space. After establishing that he didn't have a pen, I kindly loaned him one, but it didn't spur the boy into action because twenty minutes later he still hadn't put pen to paper. When I tried to chivvy him along, the pupil bared his teeth, thankfully still white, and radiating hostility snarled, 'I've been to the f—-ing dentist, alright.' In a state of delayed shock, the visit had obviously touched a raw canine nerve.

Another boy, unfamiliar with 'punctuality is the politeness of princes', arrived later still. He displayed great chutzpah with his excuse but a phony accent as he was trying to impersonate a New York gangster. The mobster needs to understand that 'Doll', is no substitute for 'Miss'. Reliving the Bugsy Malone production cannot go on forever and must eventually be worked out of the system. Thank goodness the mobster had not had a dental appointment or things could really have turned nasty.

In matters closer to home, it seems that my mother's grandchildren are like buses. First numero due moves to Upper Mill and before you know it, my brother's son, numero cinque, fresh out of university, is hot on her heels. No wonder there are such concerns over mass migration. My sister, with aspiring offspring in London, said, 'It's bizarre, what on earth is the attraction?' but I thought I'd keep a train station to Manchester quiet before any other cousins decide to muscle in and send the housing stock rocketing further still. However, numero cinque won't get that sinking feeling as he crosses the threshold because my brother has had the wit to oversee the house buying process at every single step. How I so wish we had only done the same!

Yours truly

Beth

Desperate Measures

29.06.19

Dear Cassie,

In the latest emergency call put through to 'parents to the rescue', a slug, still breathing, has been found on the kitchen floor. So far, it is unclear how the suspect gained entry, but a suggestion of 'dusting' for a slime trail has not been pleasantly received. Honestly, between the paltry Custard Creams and the lack of forensics, it makes one wonder if there are any perks to the job.

Alas, I don't think that the slug was targeting the PC for her green fingered credentials, not if the desperately dehydrated house plants are anything to go by, the poor things barely registering on an anhydrous scale normally reserved for school governors. Their only hope of survival is to be placed in line with a bloody great hole.

Talking of roofs, the roofing quotes have come in and it is obvious from these that roofers charge per raindrop gaining entry.

We have two options: a ghastly priced patch, or an astronomical reroof. After considering the merits of the patch (it didn't do anything for the Scotch egg or reduce your daily habit) we have decided to bite the bullet and go for the full reroof.

The PC is working out a repayment method to span the next ninety years, with a break for when she needs to save up for a holiday to Bogotá. I said to her, 'Didn't last year's trip to the Philippines in typhoon season teach you anything?' but she is a girl who takes after her father when it comes to the bargain flight.

You wouldn't catch me going to Bognor Regis, let alone Bogotá. I've always found any name containing the word bog rather coarse. It has too many connotations of the flooded boys' toilets, Stuart's misdirection across the moors and the standard response to the loan of the pen. However, the globetrotting PC commented that she wasn't going to take holiday advice from us. She bags up one ear off the pavement from a machete attack (it is a lawless place, but then again I've seen the parents) and suddenly thinks she is Colombia's answer to the cartels.

'On your head be it,' or I hope they still will be, I responded. How fortuitous that Mother's post-natal advice of keeping a baby's ears firmly tucked neatly in a bonnet for the first two years of its life, to prevent them from sticking out in a crowd, has finally come in to its own. All forms of exhibitionism were sincerely frowned upon, ears being no exception. A bonnet was also an excellent way of hiding the coppery tones of the more attention seeking baby although it did meet with resistance by the age of seven.

The moorland incident came about because unlike normal people who buy an AA Fifty Family Walks guidebook, with detailed instructions and walk length, Stuart goes for the DIY option.

Every year, in January, I get his surprise Christmas present, two Ordnance Survey maps of his choosing, bought directly from Ordnance Survey in a BOGOF offer. From my mother's perspective, the ability to read a map successfully is one of life's essentials and rates as high a skill as sixteen fifteens without fingers. It wasn't just batteries that you could get your knuckles rapped for. To get extra value for money with the Cadeau de Noel, we buy extra large versions covering a wider geographical area that when opened out on a windy day provide the paragliding experience for free.

The cartophiles in the family – map lovers to you and me – never miss an offer; moreover, they never miss an episode of the Archers and they are not even genetically linked. What my husband and mother don't seem to realise is that, nowadays, the map is to the mobile phone as the flask is to a handheld Starbucks. They are completely out of date but there are none so blind as those who will not see, especially when the wind whips up and wraps the map around the head. I'm fighting a losing battle in the modernisation stakes.

Thus, map in hand, after a folding contest that also gets the better of me (a fervent desire to rip it to shreds) and a scolding for incompetence, usually reserved for an alleged lack of spatial awareness with the 'correct' loading of the dishwasher, we began a walk in the Goyt Valley in Derbyshire, a hot spot for walkers. The clue should have been in the 'hot spot' for walkers. Walking by ourselves across a boggy moor, more space than enough to be aware of, knee deep in mud, not another human being in sight, with only an extra-large map for warmth, is not following the pack on a designated stone path. It was extremely hard going and repeated ankle spraining should not be considered part and parcel of the fun family walking experience. Thank goodness there were no sinking sands or unexploded ordnance, but I'll save the Northumberland experience and the perils of walking around Holy Island for another time.

Ordnance Survey maps can come in handy occasionally, not when lost on a walk, but in the geography classroom, their rightful home, as a backup for when a lesson plan has gone awry. 'Is it a church with spire or church with tower?' updated to, 'Is it a place of worship with spire, minaret or dome, or place of worship with tower?' always answers the prayers.

I recently had to teach a Year 7 geography lesson entitled 'Looking for Walter'. (Well, why not, we are looking for every bugger else; add him to the list.) The premise of the textbook exercise is that where we live affects our lives, from language to food, to education and so forth. Seven billion people live in the world and from a series of maps, photographs, pictures, and clues we had to determine where Walter, one of the seven-billion-member club, lived.

Finding Walter's home address should have been the climax to the lesson after travelling through continents, countries, counties, and cities and learning the differences between them. But I get the smart arse calling out 181, Anfield Road, Liverpool, as if they had scored a full house and were waiting for me hand out the prize fund alongside Jurgen

Klopp. (Don't you just love Jurgen Klopp?) A one in seven billion chance of finding something in the school setting, the only thing that has been found, and we hit the jackpot within a minute. Yet a small pair of steps in fluorescent yellow will not glow and show up in the dark.

Once the excitement had abated, a firm hand needed, the pupils were asked to draw a spider diagram giving details about where Walter lived such as in Europe, in a city, near a football ground and so on. The pupils then had to do a similar spider diagram for themselves, entitled 'Where I live'. Well, how difficult a task can that be? It was easier to locate a stranger in a heartbeat than know their own address.

'Should I put my mum's house down or my dad's?'

'Do you want the Florida holiday home?'

'Shall I put caravan because the house is being renovated?'

'Does it need a postcode?'

'We've had to move from Sussex because of my dad's job and I'm more familiar with the Sussex house and area.'

I don't give a damn, put anything down, well anything that is except vegan which doesn't really count, or that the summer solstice (a previous exercise and one where the recalcitrant pupil would not back down) is on the 33rd of the month.

At least the answers given went into an exercise book, negating the quest for the school holy grail, paper. Empty, never replenished, paper trays headed lined, plain, scrap, or in the maths room, dotty and square, are becoming all too familiar labels for my distinguishing features.

The history department provided some relief from looking

for Walter but it has its own set of problems ranging from a short shited Louis 16th (stick to myopic in future) to pheasants holding up the feudal system.

Then there is Red Lester the Great. Not royalty residing under a Leicester car park but the 'greated' cheese topping for the pizza that Grandma so admires.

As for those who dream of nothing but going on their holidays – the English department, with the endless 'marketing and design a holiday brochure' task – I have encountered a hotel advertising not only the 'b day' but 'on sweet' facilities as well. At least one child has taken notice of the word-bank wall in the food technology department, containing every word relating to the taste and texture of food except for revolting.

Words are generally useful in the diary writing process but if the history department is going to throw a dog a bone it will need to create a word-bank wall of its own.

The Year 8 pupils had to write a diary extract on the English Civil War, expressed from the point of view of either a Roundhead or a Cavalier. Don't worry; Samuel Pepys can rest easy.

'It has been announced on the radio that Charles is dead, and I am gutted.' (Royalist)

'It was mint to see Charles dead.' (Parliamentarian)

'I don't think it is right we should have to write a diary because a diary is private, and I don't let anybody read my diary.' (Neutral)

If the Royalist's extract had mentioned Charles' demise being announced over the wireless it would have been understandable, but the radio really is far too contemporary.

With the rewriting of history, I am sure it won't be long before the e-mail comes into the documentation. I can see the pupil account now. Harold lost the battle because he didn't open the e-mail to warn him of how good William was at conkering. If only he had seen it– the e-mail, not the arrow –he could have had them toughened up (the men not his conkers, risk assessment permitting) before the encounter!

It's not only reluctant diary writers that I have had to contend with recently. In a rare change to the English substitution lesson (taking a break from going on a break), I had to conduct an exercise with a Year 7 class entitled 'This is Me'. Thank goodness not 'Where I Live'.

Details such as inside leg measurement and shoe size, not the size of the mortgage and years left to run, had to be placed around an image of a unisex child. From the information gleaned I could tell you what a child had for its breakfast last Tuesday, dressed in its favourite colours, but I'm still in the dark as to whether it is a girl or boy.

The body part measurements proved somewhat divisive, battles over exaggerated size claims and eye number declining with each wield of the metre ruler. The box of small mirrors (my heart sank too), absolutely flew off the shelf, clumsy a trait to be added. The mirrors provided, to count teeth, not look for the other, showed no sign of wisdom from a department that has spent far too long sitting out in the sun.

Pulling teeth, not counting them, would have been easier than getting the pupils to answer the specific questions relating to the exercise.

Arthur, born three minutes after midnight on 1st September, couldn't comment on what he would you like to achieve before the age of twelve because he was beyond the age limit, proof of age documentation, counterfeit or otherwise, not forthcoming. And young Polly, with years still ahead of her, couldn't commit to her favourite book on the grounds 'I'm an avid reader with a spelling age of fifteen years and seven months. My junior schoolteacher described me as a voracious reader, and I love all books. And, I don't know how anyone could have a pet hate because I love all animals as much as I love books'. As for Corey the Cat Killer, little interest in literature or animal welfare, he refused to engage with the backing of his mother. 'My mum says that teachers want to know too much. I hate all cats and that's all I'm putting down because I don't see what it has got to do with you what I have in my favourite sandwich.'

It must be wonderful to teach a subject where, every lesson, you can rely upon 'just get out the pastels and smudge it, love'.

Misconceptions are as rife beyond as within the school gates, as I found out when recently visiting a bookstore to buy – or order, if they didn't stock it – one of my favourite childhood books, intended as a gift for the birthday of a friend's child. I did not expect when ascertaining, 'Do you have any Br'er Rabbit books?' to get the response, 'Is that who wrote it?'! How much despair can one get in a day?

On a cheerier note, and to stave off despondency, let's hope you are all ears to the pupil joke of the week, found in the school newsletter, not extracted under torture from the unisex child giving a body part inventory. 'How many ears did Captain Kirk have?' 'Two,' I can hear you respond, making a right pig's ear of it as I did; but the correct answer is three: the left ear, the right ear, and the final front ear! It's the way I tell them!

And it is marginally better than, 'What happened to the fella that walked into the pizzeria?' Answer, 'He topped himself.' After enduring the Year 7 pizza making exercise, why am I not surprised?! How difficult can it be to open and drain a can of pineapple rings, without the need for tetanus and preventative measures to stop the rings sliding, like bangles, down exceptionally thin (all measurements duly noted) puny arms?!

Yours truly

Beth

Not Out of the Woods

12.07.19

Dear Cassie,

The scaffolding on Meg's house has been erected and roofing will soon commence. I hope that when I go across, to oversee the start of proceedings, I will not be greeted with the usual, 'Where do you want it, love, front, back or on top?' Although I think that the roofers may have found me rather wanting when I initially asked, as any dutiful mother would, if they would be able to keep the noise down when the PC was on night duty. She needs her beauty sleep when all is said and done. Well, the two roofers looked at me as if I were incapable of working out a quarter of a tin of Heinz treacle pudding, hammering home the point that every single element of roofing involved knocking and banging. Indeed, that is why they must have the radio turned up extra loud. Well, they won't be turning it up to full volume if the PC is sleeping soundly and I am walking around, on the ground below, with a placard that says 'Silence Exams in Progress' with the last three words deleted out.

On the school front, as well as squashing, starving, and sticking the blighters to the drawing board, I can now add throttling, beating and eye poking to the list. Years of experience in the making.

Dear Mrs James,

The fastened shirt collar top button rule is ridiculous, it is choking my son. Please allow him to leave it unbuttoned so that he can breathe.

Dear Mrs James,

You have unfairly given my son fifty lines for beating an African drum, pray tell, how else was he supposed to play it?

(The music lesson, not the maths lesson, would be a start with that one.)

Dear Mrs James,

You moved our Darren next to a window with a protruding opener that nearly had his eye out when there was a skirmish. Please rebuke the boy who pushed him, and can you move him back to his original seat please?

Stuart said – I assume to take my mind off school; it is incredibly stressful getting all these letters of complaint – 'How would you like to revisit Intercourse?'

I responded, 'I can't think about that now, I'm just in the middle of doing the tea.' But he wouldn't be put off and commented that he was thinking of next June. He is a much-organised person and always does better with advanced planning. So, June it is, and I am already excited at the prospect, but the PC, upon finding out our intentions pleaded, 'Please, please, please do not send another postcard with 'I love Intercourse' emblazoned across the front, this year's was more than enough. Don't you realise that I have friends around to stay and Sarge might call in to see my new house?'.

The PC doesn't know how lucky she is that her parents are well travelled, a conscious decision after Stuart's life-threatening illnesses, and especially so when it comes to travel in the USA. We are only too pleased to share our Intercourse images with her.

Intercourse, a village in Pennsylvania, is at the heart of the Amish community in Lancaster County. Learning about the Amish way of life and culture was a fascinating experience for us and hence the reason we are making a return visit to Intercourse. There is something incredibly endearing about seeing horse drawn buggies running alongside the modern-day motor car. However, rest assured, the PC won't be receiving any more revealing Intercourse postcards from my travels now that I have found out she is mistaking them for the seasoned kiln dried log. She will have to receive holiday information in the same way as the rest of the world, in an instant telephone communiqué and forgo all good things that comes to he who waits. Nevertheless, her excitement will know no bounds when she gets the electronic image of me scaling McAfee's Knob in the Appalachian Mountains; I just hope that Stuart speeds up with his photography because at my age I can't cling on forever.

We have walked part of the Appalachian Trail before – think Bill Bryson and his book 'A Walk in the Woods', covering a whole ten miles of the two thousand, one hundred and ninety-mile hiking route, stretching from Springer Mountain in Georgia to Mount Katahdin in Maine, by ourselves. I don't know about a walk in the woods – some of the hikers on the trail could have done with a wash in the woods, they can be very ripe, and my sympathies are with the bears.

A walk in the woods wouldn't be too disagreeable in England – we are, after all, a very hygienic nation, and probably invented the flannel – but across the pond you can't see the wood for the trees, which isn't much good for those brought up with the notion that a walk with a view is the only one worth seeing. However, I couldn't share this viewpoint with the tour leader, already under severe strain, sweating cobs due to the humidity of the trees and his woollie. That's the trouble with the English mentality, always having to have a woollie to hand, just in case.

In England, the tour leader is usually very buttoned up – 'it's choking' isn't going to win me over at a Police Swearing in Ceremony – to help blend in with the crowd, but at least in America, shorts and a t shirt are climatically permitted. And let's face it, the choice of eateries, Maw's Pantry or the Fiddlin Pig with Bluegrass Barbecue are hardly going to require dress code even if the grits that gave him the ——, well let's just not go there, are off the menu.

When we were on the Appalachian Trail, we were excited to speak to anyone on the same path (geographically speaking, not the educational route), mainly so that they would be impressed by our English credentials. We had practised and practised 'howdie', which, tellingly, still comes out as 'How do you do?' in the wash.

'That sounds like a very Yorkshire accent, if ever I've heard one,' said the very first girl we met (no relation of Mrs Prendergast), 'I'm from Accrington Stanley.'

Honest to goodness, I'm haunted by the other side; is there simply no escape? So, I suggested to hubby that next time we should go for the Tennessee salutation, we are state lingual after all, and try 'How's youse all doin, y'all?' in the hope we might meet an actual, bonafide American, not a Lancastrian on the wrong path. 'Best not,' was the reply. If he didn't mutter under his breath, loud enough to be heard, that greeting option would still be open to us, but when the good old country boys follow up, 'How's youse all doin y'all?' with 'are youse all here to see kin?' and it gets the response 'Not if they blinking (could have been a more 'choice' word, not found in Mother's dictionary) look like you,' it is not going to win over any new international friends. We obviously need to spend more time across the Pennines if we are to get a handle on the hillbilly line.

Talking of hillbillies, the Tennesseans have some very strange names for dining establishments. High on the Hog, Smoke Signals, Liquids and Solids, Pickled Pig, Red Neck Bistro, Critters, Lord of the Fries, Moose Munch, Squeaky Rail Diner and 'Stuff and Stuff' (hardly the gentility of the 'Sip and Savour') might be suitable for those lacking a flannel but for those with a woollie, just in case, the more refined dining experience is required.

I commented to a husband in the throes of living the dream and throwing away the shackles of his reserved, stiff upper lip Englishness, 'Neither the wearing of your cowboy, trucker, or Casey Jones hat is going to get me through the door of any of those establishments. What's more, before you purchase any more inappropriate American head gear (really, his head shape is not suited to the national costume) you need to give serious consideration to luggage weight limits, I'm not running an 'all hat and no knickers' packing operation here, particularly when he is the first to complain.

Talking of hats, I observed a young woman the other day wearing the obligatory ubiquitous woolly pompom hat (it is strange how pupils, upon leaving school, lose the ability to rebel and rail against the standardised uniform of the day), with a body warmer, shorts and flip flops to complete the look. I might adore the word pompom (possibly originating from the French word pompon, but we can't hold that against it); however, I do not believe in mixing and matching the winter and summer wardrobe, especially when my body is designed with one thermoregulatory centre, not two. Surely other people feel the cold all over; it can't just be me.

The PC has added something called 'loungewear' (Kyle's influence again) to her wardrobe; it goes without saying that we won't be encouraging any of those 'slouching about' ways, with or without the persuasive English argument. Yes, I have been subjected to the persuasive English writing task, yet again. Things are never that bad they can't get worse. This time, the statement to argue over was 'The majority of time spent at school is wasted'. Agree or disagree.

Someone has clearly been on the ball in setting that statement and from my own perspective I wholeheartedly agree: most of the time spent at school is wasted. In fact, I would go as far as to say that it is scandalously wasted, particularly by the professional pencil sharpener. When I say professional pencil sharpener, I'm not referring to the desktop kind with five settings of sharpness grade, durable mechanism, and rotary crank handle, to help sharpen any pencils or crayons quickly and with almost any effort. No, with crank handle in hand, maximum effort expended, the true professional can spend all lesson long making repeated visits to the rubbish bin to work on their pencil shaving technique, from the gossamer to the full log. The process can also provide the opportunity to meet up with likeminded individuals for a little chinwag to share and develop other diversionary tactics. It's not as if a spot of whittling, now the wooden desk has been replaced by durable melamine, can help to concentrate the mind. But all is not lost: there is always the school nurse and her stress ball to fall back upon, or over, for the pupil handed the school bin exclusion notice. True stress, however, is when the manipulator of the stress ball can masterfully get it to explode over the entire classroom. Have you any idea how difficult, without access to a dustpan and brush in an English room setting, kinetic sand, the stress ball filling, is to clear? Nearly as tricky as scraping solidified molten plastic from the inside of a desecrated oven (sacred to Mrs P), followed by a washing down with school detergent so diluted that a farting minnow could make more bubbles and headway. Nothing but one wretched lather after another.

Yours truly

Beth

PS I do wish that creative writing, not persuasive writing, would feature more prominently on the English syllabus, both here and in the States.

The crustacean (the nearest Americans get to vegetarianism) may be the only item featuring on the Maine menu but surely there is a sign writer out there who can creatively come up with a more original name for the Maine general store (every single last one of them) than the Lobstore.

A Deep Depression

10.09.19

Dear Cassie,

There are certain combinations that should never be put together: actors working with animals and children, redheads and the wearing of pink (not a stated law but some things do not need putting into words), the sock and the male sandal (rubbed little toes, sore pads and blisters don't get the sympathy vote with me when I am aspiring to the Starbucks look), children at break time in unsupervised classrooms (the state of the floor, the state of the ceiling, the state of walls, the teacher's desk and the paper-jammed printer) and finally, but most importantly of all, the use of not one, but two liquid measurements in the school cooking process.

It is muffin making time again, Groundhog Day, in a never-ending cyclic process that requires the use of sunflower oil and milk in the baking method. However, if a broken leg with better odds than the annual school ski trip is to be avoided, never the twain shall meet.

In theory, there should not have been a problem because, yet again, at the start of the new school year, I diligently demonstrated the muffin making process, giving clear and precise instructions on ingredients, quantities, method, cooking time and oven temperature. Safe transportation of liquids from home to school was also discussed verbatim, with lots of technical advice such as screw the lid on tightly and give it plenty torque, a more scientific term than 'wellie,' for the trained science teachers amongst us. It's no good letting all my training go to waste and I wanted Mrs P to know that I can torque the torque with the best of them.

I had bargained for the usual disparity in household scales but not the gender fluidity of the humble measuring jug, still debating whether to come out as a fluid millilitre or a fluid ounce.

The sunflower oil, dispensed from the micro pipette to the gallon drum, not the wavering measuring jug, should have been beaten with the milk and eggs, before mixing with the dry ingredients, not left to float on top of the batter like engine oil in an iridescent puddle. Pouring oil on troubled waters is an understatement. And how difficult can it be for a parent to provide a muffin case, a couple of sizes up from a standard bun case, not six sizes down from a thimble? The recipe was for a dozen, but one girl managed a gross. Had you had my upbringing you would know, along with the number of feet, yards and furlongs that make up a mile. Education in the Cousteau era.

The number of chocolate chips – 'forbidden fruit tastes sweetest' – thrown into the mix must have numbered a gross squared (a dozen to the power four, although in your case, maths not a strong suit, I'm not sure that will help), providing any number of reasons to account for the density of the muffins. The perfect muffin should spring to the touch, not provide armaments for the salvo of the English civil war cannon.

To provide some light relief from the working out of taxing mathematical problems (all workings out to be clearly shown) and committing to memory the new definition of a baker's dozen, I have decided to write a new weekly nature column entitled 'Nature's Latest Nuisance to Invade my Personal Space'. (It worked for the resource ladies.) To add to the usual suspects – don't let me get started on felines, and their incomprehensible vile shit (really, what do they put in Kitty Cat?) – I am adding the ladybird and the sparrow hawk.

As a lover of roses (Joie de Vivre favourite but like all in blush pink) I have welcomed the ladybird into my garden, to dine out on the aphids sucking the life out of my roses, not to take up a permanent house residency. We now have a ladybug infestation with the blasted bugs residing inside my wooden window frames. Yes, I know, more updating needed to get the uPVC look but annual treatment with wood stain, as in the parental guide to good property maintenance (if you're going to do a job, do it right) and thirty years on the buggers still refuse to rot. I am my own worst enemy.

And if my mother thinks that the crow's table manners leave a lot to be desired, wait until she has a sparrow hawk swoop on down at speed and snatch a little sweetie (not Paul Martin but we can but hope), one of my freshly replete, delightful little garden birds. Talk about biting the hand that feeds you; I was mortified. I should have left a chocolate chip muffin on the bird table, tarred and feathered with some of Honeypot's finest for disguise. That would have stopped the tertiary consumer in the food chain in its tracks as it plummeted from the sky.

At school, the pupils continue to make heavy weather of things on several fronts, especially warm ones. Conducting lessons outdoors in a heatwave, no matter how high the demand and expectation, is never the way to take the heat out of the situation, contrary to popular belief. Some faint-hearted souls use the weather as an excuse for sitting with their head between their knees all day long. Where's the backbone? They need to steel themselves, as I must, listening to pupils' experiences of the weather.

'When we were on holiday in Turkey, Miss, all exclusive, eat and drink as much as you like – do you do all exclusive, Miss? – it was that hot that my Grandma had to lay stripped off on the bed with the electric fan next to her so that she didn't die.'

'Is that so, Sheriden?'

'It is, Miss.'

A naked granny with a fan is probably a better look than for some I could mention, overcome by heat exhaustion in the US.

Lacking a camel, turban, and the name of Lawrence, I declined the opportunity to climb the Great Sand Dunes in Colorado; pity the other half of the party didn't heed my advice. Have you ever seen anyone, upon their return, look as if they have been pegged out by the Apaches? It is not a good look. However, overheating in the USA has not been restricted to the desert. At a restaurant in Philadelphia, we were given 'iced water to go'. Don't know if this was given as an incentive to lure a man pinioned under the weight of a Philly Cheese Steak from his seat or because 'Smokey Bear' was signalling that we were the imminent fire threat.

Self-combustion was a distinct possibility at the Lassen Volcanic Park in California, outside temperature Saharan. We should have been the paid feature; we were emitting more steam than the mud pots. The only atmospheric conditions in the world to make sitting in an airless, overcrowded school hall assembly, tediously running over, look enticing, with or without the prospect of being skittled by the mass fainting domino effect.

The school day would be so much easier (heatwaves and 'blowing a gale' conditions excepting – the behaviour barometer needle swinging from lethargic to manically wild) if pupils had a better understanding of high-pressure and low-pressure systems and that in a deep depression, rain bearing cloud requires a coat. That said, I'm sure even our weather challenged pupils would realise that sun cream does not stick to wet skin, unlike their American cousins in Cape Cod who needed it spelling out on the weather channel. 'Precipitation levels 100 per cent. UV levels, sun cream does not apply.'

However, in Acadia National Park in Maine, my favourite state, Smokey Bear's fire risk of 'moderate' was rather optimistic in a flood, but then again, the topic of probability is widely misunderstood.

Pupils should be put through the wringer for soaking up and revelling in so much lunchtime fun, not drip drying over the radiators, tables, chairs, floor, ceiling (a similar action to that of a wet dog) and their own soggy, saturated, disintegrating schoolwork. Although credit where credit's due, the pupils wouldn't be fazed by a watery abyss, when venturing from the car in Maine, shouting out with parting shot, 'If I'm not back in five minutes, Carruthers, find me some dry socks!'

I have been put through the wringer myself – being hung out to drip dry is too good for those that commit the cardinal sin of ringing up their mother during the omnibus edition of the Archers. 'Caller stopped breathing' doesn't constitute grounds for such an intrusion, although the undisguised annoyance did fairly take my breath away.

My son has also been complaining, this time, that I use the computer keyboard keys to write to you inappropriately. It transpires that I am using the keyboard as a typewriter (sharp as a tack, that lad) and bashing the keys so hard that the clickety clack is going right through his head. Call me old fashioned, but I was home schooled in the art of QWERTY – times tables weren't the only item on the agenda – and subjected to the blindfold (a lost educational tool) which puts an entirely different emphasis on the matter.

Hubby, aka The Princess and the Pea, is having trouble accepting brand new, best quality Marks and Spencer pyjamas in his life. He doesn't cope well with change. I've told him that they will soften with time; anyone would think I had deliberately set out to give him friction burns. If he doesn't get a grip soon, he'll find himself tied to the bed, all bows and ribbons, in the Cavalier silk range.

As for the PC, she is put out with me, without me even speaking, powers of clairvoyance so strong she apparently knows what I am thinking. Good. I thought the new house, Arctic Fox, and log burner (with logs and fire lighting postcards) were precursors to a husband not the designer dog. There's no need to rely on telepathy to get that message through, I'll put it in writing – 'I will not be crossing the Pennines to walk a Cockapoo at the toot of the police whistle.' No wonder the country is in the state it is in when the police dog is chosen for being cute and adorable. The criminals must be quaking in their boots at the thought of 'K9 Cuddly' straining at the leash to frolic and rollick and lick them into submission.

So, already in the bad books for stating, 'No, your father is not ready for retirement and wanting to take up 'daddy, doggie day care,' I took the opportunity to add, 'Try air in the tyres when the air pressure warning light comes on, not ringing us for advice at all hours!'

Yours truly

Beth

Falling on Deaf Ears

31.10.19

Dear Cassie,

When I instructed Stuart to find alternative accommodation to the Lake District pub short of the full English, the Royal Lancashire Infirmary didn't immediately spring to mind. I should have known better when the meals and boarding are free, no coupon or advanced booking required of any kind.

On our latest trip to the Lakes, for a week's walking holiday at October half term, I had a spot of bother caused by neither the effects of the lite bite nor the full bite. I fell, not with dignity on the fells, but indignantly in the shower. No need for too many details (how tiresome is listening to others' mishaps or medical histories) although I would like to point out that the maddening modern-day salutation of 'Are you alright?' which has insidiously replaced 'hello' is futile when the person giving the greeting invariably walks past without awaiting the answer. My mother never allows the questioner to get away with it, providing a full blown, detailed reply. So, to sum up the situation as succinctly as possible, and not make the same mistake, I was diagnosed, after a hair-raising ride in the ambulance, with a small bleed on the brain. I had hit my head with the force of a minor car crash on a piece of sanitaryware that had no right to be sitting right next to the shower.

The brain injury was compounded further when the stocky, rather swarthy, young male nurse in charge of my care in the casualty department, before admittance to the acute medical assessment ward, asked me where I was from. Despite my dazed, somewhat befuddled, state I managed to proudly utter 'Yorkshire'.

'Where's that?' the nurse, who looked like a prime candidate for an extra in the Breaking Bad movie on the wrong side of the border, asked. 'Where's that?' I repeated incredulous, thinking the injury must be serious, and prompting a fit of choking requiring the Real McCoy medical professional to perform the Heimlich manoeuvre. The choking was on a par with that reserved for the American waitress (in need of her cards) ascertaining 'Would you like to see the seniors' menu, ma'am?'

I don't think that I've ever been in such a state of shock and disbelief. Not that it engendered any sympathy from offspring, more concerned with the state of my undress, than a nurse, not long to these shores, unable to cross the county line with fajitas.

The PC commented she hoped the hotel supplied bath and not just hand towels and the lodger chipped in that a hastily pulled down shower curtain would not have had enough material to hand. Even my own mother, oblivious to the fact I was punch-drunk from Yorkshire not featuring on the worldwide geography syllabus, or that I'd been offered half rations across the pond, seemed to think I'd been remiss for getting into a shower naked, when one should always be prepared for all eventualities. Yes, well, we don't all operate the flannel method of washing via the hand basin only, with discreet lifting of garments because of never having learned to swim. There is more than one reason for steering clear of rivers and valley bottoms and it's not always linked to the exorbitant cost of the flooded homes house insurance policy.

Anyway, away from the purgatory, noise, sleep deprivation and torture methods of the hospital ward – I've had more light shone into my eyes than the modern foreign language department can provide – the PC has been rather touchy.

All I said, to trigger a raw nerve, was that the younger of the two roofers was rather nice looking. Obviously, the older one has had more time to succumb to the elements, but all is not lost because I am sure my expert, Mateo, could supply some sort of male face cream, at a ghastly cost. The PC needs to keep her eye out, or upwards; the biological clock is ticking.

Casting her eye around the police force is clearly not providing the answer. I was knocked for six when the PC said, 'Don't you know the saying, 'join the force get a divorce'?' I certainly do not know such a saying, how would I, when divorce is strictly forbidden in my family and where no divorce has ever taken place. And we're not even Catholic.

'You've made your bed, now lie in it.' And I should know, upside down at the pillow end, when I played the game of flopping backwards as a child and broke two bed legs. I was left for a week with the blood coursing to my head to convey the folly of that manoeuvre; can you imagine the punishment if I were to dare to say I'm thinking of leaving hubs, it would be more than the blindfold I can tell you.

As a family we are serious collectors of the wedding anniversary certificate with special award ceremonies, food provided, not a miserly Custard Cream, for those achieving silver, pearl, ruby, gold, and diamond status with special merit for those attempting the sapphire award.

In order that the PC can start her own collection of certificates, I have started watching 'The Force' to see if I can pick out any lookers and make a note of their collar numbers, but it's no mean feat. I'm beginning to see the nature of the beast. I don't even think there is anyone who would take your fancy – and you're not that fussy.

Knowing that you shouldn't judge a book by its cover, I've started looking for other attributes such as athleticism and intellect, but when they get to a job it's more of an amble than a full-on chase, followed by the stunning intellectual insight, 'it's a dog job is this, it's not for us'. Well, I could have told them that before they joined, as I told my own daughter, but would she listen.

Listening is the greatest skill that has been lost in schools over the last thirty years, listening being dispensed with in favour of incessant chattering. Chattering through the reading of the pupil daily bulletin in form time, chattering in assemblies, with or without a guest speaker, chattering in the library, chattering during lesson explanations, chattering during science practicals, cooking practicals, power points, class demonstrations (the model penis excepting, size generating rapt awe and an inability to speak) and finally chattering during practising the St John's ambulance kiss of life technique. Honestly, you could draw your last breath waiting for the school pupil to finish a conversation. And now, even more staggering than the diminishing status of God's own county, I can add gabbing on a mobile phone, at ten o'clock at night, on a shared hospital ward, by garrulous grown adults who should know better, and for whom the guillotine, if ever found, would not do justice.

I think that a time and motion study, or better still, surveillance camera, would throw disturbing light on the endless hours of lost learning time through idle chit chat and lack of focus. But these things can never be mentioned because other colleagues have no issues with the 'fantastic', implying they are far more engaging in their teaching methods than I. Alas, it is always these colleagues whose classes, from a supply point of view, are the most challenging to teach, with rowdy behaviour and a resounding inability to listen.

Tolerance levels amongst the teaching fraternity vary widely, but when you can engage with a form, without sanction, for betting openly on playing cards for money, or discussing in detail the likely odds of a football team winning, you know that you are on the way to the top. Successfully explaining Boyle's Law is not in the same league as 'Do you think the game will be three two to Barca tonight?'. Getting across difficult concepts can't always be fun and light and we could all engender a good rapport, if we were hedging our bets at the bookies.

When back up has been needed, to help control an unruly class, or a seriously misbehaving individual, it has been in noticeably short supply. (Remember, I am paid for the privilege.) And to be honest, it doesn't help when the 'on duty' member of the emergency team, supposedly riding to my rescue, greets the class with, 'Hi guys, what's all this about when you are so well behaved for me.' That's it, use the self congratulatory approach to promote 'how great thou are', diminishing, yet further, the standing of the supply teacher stood directly in front of the class. Although naturally, I lose confidence in any teacher's abilities, senior level or otherwise, for restoring law and order and addressing misbehaviour at the point of 'hi'. Moreover, there was also a time when 'cheers' was reserved solely for the clinking of glasses, not the hard word.

Talking of the football scores – sport really isn't my thing, unless running out of the school gates quicker than Santa and his reindeers on the Christmas Jumper Santa fundraising dash counts – the PC has been policing a number of Premier League football matches.

For some bizarre reason, people at football matches, gay parades, festivals, and the like, want their mugshot taken voluntarily, standing next to a police officer. No need to work up a sweat, just get the Kodak out. I said I hoped to goodness it wasn't her thumpers that had caught the attention for the family photograph album, but Meg replied that it was just the norm and more about the hat. Well, I rest my case about declining standards, overfamiliarity (familiarity breeds contempt) and a general lack of respect, although at least she has a hat when she is tapped on top of the head – all I ever get is, 'I'm only trying to be friendly'.

Yours truly

Beth

Going Backwards

03.11.19

Dear Cassie,

How many gnawed plastic cocoa tub lids do you think I will have to write off before the sweet-toothed rodent reads the highlighted message, in ultra-bright neon colours, to clear off and look for a soporific night cap in another joint? Mouse Membership Expired. The intrusion has happened again, this time under the very nose of the doorman supposedly dealing with the situation. A wiry weasel (mouse hunting skills eminently superior to those of the illiterate, trespassing, contemptuous cats belonging to neighbours near and far) tears across the front patio every afternoon, out of the bordering dry-stone wall, with a dead mouse clasped in its jaws. Very impressive, an extremely civic minded response (not that I'd wish to shake hands with it), but we need a weasel for the night shift, not one counting the calories at weight watchers for weasels, refusing the chance to dine out on a delicious, sweet mouse.

In addition to an image conscious weasel (the drawbacks of social media) we have got new neighbours, a middle-aged couple, from London. Enough said. The ladies in resources won't be going into overdrive, any time soon, with the photocopying button, unless that is, the school has begun administering nuisance neighbour certificates.

The washing left out on the line all day long should have been a portent of what was to come but the PC thinks I am too judgemental and that having the washing dried, ironed, and put away in a three-hour period is a syndrome not a speciality. It's a necessity if you live next door to a 'burner', but my daughter can't get past the concept of the untraceable phone.

Regrettably, the new neighbours to the rear of the house are of the same ilk as those living to the front of the house, 'hen lovers,' although in this case, gabbling geese, guinea fowl and a wild pheasant have joined the shindig. And they don't love them that much because the hen coop (rats will follow) has been placed nearer to my garden seating area than their own. This is highly distressing, particularly when I have given up the chocolate biscuit in favour of the Marks and Spencer cocoa dusted Belgian truffle. It's not a widely known diet but cocoa dusted truffles are easier, or should be, to hide than family sized packs of biscuits and are part of my cunning plan to keep the lodger off the scent, not rodents amassing by the hour.

Lamentably, the man of the house was unapologetic when asked to retrieve his member from my garden, despite an exact description of the offending specimen. (I'm now fully up to speed and conversant with criminal investigative procedures and the poultry identity parade.)

Colour – white; size – nothing to write home about;

identifying features – red comb and wattle, scaly legs (mother's favourite expression, 'couldn't stop a pig in a ginnel', does not apply), simple expression and wearing feathers – not that I want to give the misleading impression that Honeypots has been shitting in my garden!

Regardless of such a disturbing image (blame the English Department, they are obsessed with imagery), the suspect was so relaxed in its new, tastefully planted surroundings, managing to taste more plants than quartered biscuit crumbs on offer to the lunch-deprived pupil, recently released from the store cupboard, that it had the brass neck, or some other such body part, to lay an egg. I am quite beside myself; it is not over egging the pudding (contrary to Mrs P's assessment) to say that eggs, one way or another, are becoming the bane of my life.

I need a place to sit and relax, not tread on eggshells, when I get home from school, namely, to counter the effects of passive farting, the elephant in the classroom. School air is so potent due to rampant, trumping teenagers that Porton Down could bottle it.

The German Government, I recently read in a newspaper article, are to counteract this teaching hazard by pumping perfumes into classrooms to boost pupils' concentration and energy levels. Anything to mask the stink. Six schools have been given the task of trialling the scent of lavender, grapefruit, orange, lemon, pomegranate, and cedar wood oil, which is being sprayed through nozzles next to the blackboard (outdated choice) every two hours. Any change in mood, attitude to learning or rise in pupil activity (don't

forget the sneezing, eyes watering and contact urticaria), will
be researched and monitored by scientists and teachers in a
yearlong project to find the ideal 'learning scent'.

What do we have at our disposal, an imaginary peg, and
the nonexistent scent of Vapona! I'm yet to forgive the
kamikaze bluebottle dive-bombing the precious milk stocks
or the British Government for doing away with the actual
peg, in a bid to maximise classroom space. It can't just be
my rotator cuff under strain when pupils are mobile coat
hooks, and the average sized school bag can accommodate
its owner plus Shergar.

The Americans, on the other hand, are ruthless when it
comes to insecticide, but less troubled with shoulder pain
as they are a very litigious nation.

This year, whilst on holiday in Maine, we were distinctly
underprepared; a discreet dab of aromatic citronella on the
wrists is not going to do the trick when under severe attack
from savage mosquitoes mistaking us for the full English.
In desperation, upping the dose to a light dab behind the
ears made no difference, even if it is the courteous method
of fragrance application for those with allergic rhinitis and
should become a legal requirement of anyone attending
the theatre. (I've paid for more performances than I have
actually seen.)

To counter the attack, we sought assistance at Walgreens,
the chemist, where we were advised to purchase bug spray
with 'd'. Not sure what the 'd' stands for, but death to the
sprayer before the bug would seem the most likely option.
The pollen count attached to the BBC weather forecast might

have the British reaching for the tissues (sadly, no longer manly, men having gone out of fashion), but it doesn't have the sting of an American 'skeeter' forecast where the highest concentration of skeeters is actually classified as gross (more skeeters than chocolate chips) and the remedy leaves one smarting.

In home news, my sister, brother-in-law, niece, and niece's boyfriend have been to visit following my head injury. I did stress that there was no need; my mother has already done a full mental acuity test (no need to be made to read, out loud, an extract from the Power Station Quarterly) after dissatisfaction with the rigour of the one given in the Casualty department. Losing your marbles not allowed. Why, the first thing my mother does upon waking up from a general anaesthetic is her twelve times tables followed by a rendition of Alfred Lord Tennyson's The Charge of the Light Brigade. 'Theirs not to reason why.'

At the time of the incident, I found the hospital test quite onerous but have since come to realise its limitations. 'Go backwards from one hundred, subtracting seven each time' won't separate the wheat from the chaff in anyone aged under thirty, unless the hospital is checking if the patient is sufficiently alert to work out the answers on their mobile phone.

Toutefois, retour à mes visiteurs, my niece's boyfriend is French (it will take time), and a vegan (even longer) and it is the first time we have met him. My sister said, 'Don't worry; we have warned him that you are a bit odd, even without the head injury.'

What an unbelievable cheek (she must be taking lessons from the short shited American waitress), so I retorted, 'I've already promised you, for the sake of entente cordiale, I'll stick to a pronunciation of Erique, instead of a broad Yorkshire Eric, even though I've never liked gargling when speaking.' I don't know why she's so flustered; I'm hardly likely to try out 'Voulez-vous un cupcake ou 'boone Eric?' in my best Inspector Clouseau, when most of the baking ingredients have been barred from the baking process.

'Oh, I'm not referring to your appalling French accent,' was the reply, 'more that you wince every time you have to present one cheek for a greeting, let alone two.' You're darn tootin, consider it a legacy from being forced to kiss elderly relatives as a child and ending up being scarred for life.

Before Eric with an acute accent over the E came on the scene, Stuart held the title for the most exotic family member (chilli con carne yet to be experienced – a long standing issue predating Mrs P and even when it was, the life-threatening chilli beans were dispensed with for the more trusted baked), although thankfully, the people of Darlington didn't subscribe to kissing both cheeks.

However, when we recently had a guided tour of Belsay Hall Gardens in Northumberland and the guide asked us where we were from, before I had the chance to answer Yorkshire, 'County Durham' was fiercely and proudly shouted out, as if soft, southerly Yorkshire, overrun with Londoners, had suddenly gone out of fashion. It's funny how things can soon become a trend. Some people simply don't realise on which side their bread is buttered. A spot of concussion might help bring him to his senses.

In the latest emergency call, put through to parents living counties apart, the PC's washing machine has broken down with her full kit inside (as if we haven't heard that one before). I thought, I hope she's not expecting me to send a note of excuse to the Chief Constable because I don't condone such behaviour. Talk about airing your smalls in public. I've made it clear to the PC that if she is going to send in a forged note on my behalf, to have the good sense to access the dictionary first. There is such a thing as a mini dictionary; it doesn't necessarily have to be housed in a glass case.

Dear Miss,

Colin carnt do P.E. His got a sower ancul.

Mum.

Take it from me; the Chief Constable will be adept at spotting a counterfeit a mile away.

Nonetheless, my advice to the PC went down like a lead balloon, although not as fast as my next suggestion of shouting repeatedly and loudly at the washer to open its eyes and not to go to sleep. I'm very au fait with resuscitation techniques these days and my French would appear to be on the up too. Although I'm not totally convinced 'I see you like bric-a-brac', delivered in a smouldering voice, is terribly complimentary in French.

So, before I get totally distracted, the PC shirtily demanded the immediate presence of County Durham man, with toolbox in hand, to ride to the rescue and mend the washing machine. However, there was no need for a spanner in the works. It transpired that she had never read the washer's maintenance advice and cleaned the wretched filter. I could literally run my fingers down the interactive board in exasperation.

The lodger, another not naturally drawn to the knick-knack, has also been somewhat put out with me, using an aggrieved and accusatory tone to complain I'd tossed his cell down like Miss Marple. Well, there have been some very strange scents emanating from his bedroom and I don't think they are necessarily the scents of cedar oil to help increased learning activity. As I constantly remind him, when he gets his own home he can do as he pleases, so long as it includes the use of an ironing board (the PC's is still in its cellophane wrapper twelve months after Christmas presentation – is it any wonder there's no husband in sight?) but in mine, he needs to come up smelling of roses.

Yours truly

Beth

PS After meticulous research, and the ability to follow a classification key in biology, another waning tool, I have identified the illegal migrant in my garden as a Leghorn, not a 'chance your arm' Legover.

Leghorn chickens, I am reliably informed by the internet, are 'adventurous, spirited, and wonderful egg layers. (You don't say.) The Leghorn chickens' egg laying prowess, savvy attitudes and bold personalities made them the most common pure-bred fowl in Australia in the early to mid-1900s.'

Yes, and Australia will not be far enough on the convict ship, for its fowl deeds or those of its scurrilous owner!

Low in Spirits

08.12.19

Dear Cassie,

Unsurprisingly, to the organised person in possession of a calendar, Christmas is making its creeping annual appearance again. The event always seems to catch my mother unawares, leaving her Christmas card writing to the very last minute. There are so many crossings out in her address book that there is the added burden of working out if a replacement, in the long term, would give value for money, despite gaining marks for improved presentation.

The PC, advent calendar to the rescue, picture only – breakfast standards and dental hygiene should always be rigorously enforced, especially when I'm providing the calendar – has decided to get in early and e-mail (is nothing sacred) a list of the surprise Christmas presents that she would actually like, preferably before January. Can't think why I have never thought of a leather wallet for the warrant card before, I must be losing my touch. I'd rather assumed the speeding fines covered the cost of accoutrements.

From the seasonally sublime to the ridiculous, the Shit Sues, Dexter the Dalmatian's replacements, two for the price of one, are marvellously sporting their Christmas jumpers. Ruby in red and Bella in blue. I think you would like the cut of their jib. No doubt the Rubellas (no forethought of name planning) are being treated to a little doggie bone, one behind every window to go with their fancy knits. The PC certainly likes to labour that she is the last bastion of the non-treat advent calendar. By the way, do you happen to know what the cut off age is for supplying adult daughters with the obligatory advent calendar?

In an ever-changing world, it's not just the standard communications with Santa going up the chimney, or knits that will never see full wear; the physical wedding invitation has also gone by the board. Some good friends of ours have been discombobulated (the French may have pompon and bric-a-brac but we've some good ones too) by the e-mail wedding invitation.

The wedding, their first gay wedding, with a lady-lady partnership, has got them in a spin on all counts – what to wear, what to eat, how to be a wild thing, particularly at their age. But Stuart, reading glasses at the ready, realised that the being 'wild' referred to wilding, the latest buzz word to help reduce the carbon footprint. If my mother's worried about the lack of a creamy chicken vol-au-vent, or the Scotch oeuf, at a possible family celebration in France – apparently the Frenchman distressingly told her he feels very French – wait until she's asked to plant a tree, in her best heels and wedding finery, following a wedding ceremony conducted in a copper mine in Coniston in the Lake District, to negate the wedding's carbon footprint. And I wouldn't suggest the wearing of white, not with an after-ceremony bonfire. I'll never think of a campfire (no matter how much the PC enjoyed Scouts, with the Explorer of the Year award tucked under her bulging belt) in the same light.

Fortunately, problems around the wedding gift were less onerous because altruistically and refreshingly, instead of demands of payment for the maxi moon, the e-mail suggested a choice of four charities. Well, if the Coniston Mountain Rescue Service team doesn't come top of the class, I don't know who would, although as I suggested to our friends, upfront payment with their names emblazoned across the donation would probably be best.

Ergo, with the wedding gift sorted and the suggestion of marshmallows on a stick for the homemade biting on (just in case the jacket potatoes are as sparse as a custard cream at a swearing in ceremony), the only thing left to muse over was what to wear. But as with your funeral notification, the ever-thoughtful couple's e-mail provided full details. 'Bright colours only please' – it's not just funerals cornering the market in colour, these days – 'we especially have a thing for high vis.'

'High-vis,' I choked, in a manner worthy of swallowing the seniors menu, when my daughter is unknowingly drawing attention to herself, in public, from dawn to darkest night (depending on the shift pattern) in a luminous jacket, with enough vis to dazzle and attract moths of any persuasion to the ever-shining light. If that isn't a good reason to transfer to plain clothes, I don't know what is, with the added bonus that the lacklustre jacket might actually fit. She needs to cut her cloth. Police officers may be adept at licking the point of the pencil, before taking down details of 'build' in the notebook, but if the lead given to the tailoring department ends up being blown up out of all proportion, there's little to be said for the skill. And these things are never lost (no matter where I tell her to hide it), particularly when they come under the Geoff Capes label. Our only hope is the school's textiles technology department (sewing), with its obsession for 'upcycling'. But then again, it's always easier to sew something that has been partly made than start a project from scratch. If that department can't be called upon to deftly transform a superfluous jacket with salacious connotations into a thousand and one, glow in the dark condoms, then there will never be light at the end of the tunnel!

Sticking with the school scene, but not technology's relentless marketing and branding efforts, with endless logo designs and slogans to help promote their handmade products (light at the end of the tunnel will take some beating, hand me more stars), I received a letter of apology from a pupil this week which makes a refreshing change. Certain ungrateful family members could do to follow suit; advent calendars can't always be a box of chocolates. As a result, I thought that I would share with you the rare occurrence of a pupil owning up and taking responsibility for their actions.

Dear Mrs James,

I don't no what came over me. I don't normally behave like that. It is becos I have lost my grandmar and I carn't sleep. I've been very upset. I'm very sorry. I will never get into a water fight again even though I didn't start it and it wasn't my fault. I will never do anything like that again becos it isn't me. I no it was dangerous because you slipped but please don't tell my parents becos they are very upset as well that we have lost grandmar.

If grannies weren't being passed from pillar to post, families would stand a greater chance of not losing them, wouldn't you say?

Some years ago, when I was teaching a lesson on death and bereavement in RPSE, a young man by the name of Perkins, surname not first name, contrary to the latest fad, asked to be excused because he was terribly upset over his grandfather's death and the lesson would be too upsetting for him. As a sympathetic, empathetic, peripatetic person (the last one is reserved for the pupil trying to escape the lesson by way of the private music lesson), I granted permission for Perkins to leave the lesson and sit quietly in the library. Here he would be able to have a private moment, nose buried in 'Where's Wally' not Beowulf (pupils and the supply teacher alike, drawing the short straw, when they don't possess the Anglo-Saxon ear), until I could speak to him, one to one. Upon doing so, I elicited that the grandfather had died when Perkins was a baby, yet despite thirteen intervening years, he still hadn't come to terms with the loss. By the time I'd done with him, he knew about loss, loss of his lunch hour, expeditiously sentenced for three days on the trot.

As per usual, RPSE had put the cart before the horse, starting with the despatched before the hatched and matched with confirmation featuring somewhere in between. When we eventually got round to the hatched, one young man was particularly excited because he had just attended his baby cousin's Christening. There's nothing like the firsthand account to bring a topic to life. But the boy's sum contribution, no mention of fonts, vicars, godparents, candles, prayers, baptism water or signs, was that his baby cousin had been christened Blake Adam Dent and how good those initials would look when the baby was old enough to get his arm in print.

At the mention of the name Blake, a lachrymose girl, between contagious fits of weeping, sobbed that her grandma had lost Mr Blake, making a refreshing change to the usual pattern of things. I do wish that pupils wouldn't try to revisit a topic when I've already moved on and the school librarian has indicated the library seating area is full to capacity. I don't have the patience, especially when I've sensitively established that Mr Blake has been lost from the leash, not this mortal coil. It's enough to turn you to drink, but after journeying through every ceremony and festival known to the major religions, RPSE celebrate the end of the pilgrimage (all roads lead to Mecca) with the mocktail, the alcohol-free, spiritless cocktail. Basically, it's a marginally less astringent version of the fruit fusion, with a dash to the full bottle of cochineal, glace cherry on a stick and jaunty paper umbrella, stylishly served in the slender stemmed, delicate, fragile flute. More family heirlooms (the cut glass trifle dish priceless) in shards, requiring compensation, to add to the ever-growing dry-cleaning bill.

If Mr Blake, is looking for a new home to bed down, he

needs to look no further than a new addition to my Christmas tree. I've blotted my copy book by purchasing a tree skirt, an upturned, whitewashed wicker basket, designed to hide the base of the tree. My first and last attempt at interior design as the only possibility of getting it into the loft for storage is if Gareth barrels on by. The skirt would not only satisfy Honeypot's fervent desire for 'a wicker basket, suitable for the small dog or cat please', but accommodate six corpulent persons minimum, with luggage, scaled up to trunks, for the hot air balloon ride. I've been duped more spectacularly than by 'prostrate with grief' Perkins following in the footsteps of Queen Victoria. Stuart, with strong reproof, will probably have me writing a letter of apology, when I dare to launch the unveiling, followed by a lecture on the merits and value of red crepe paper.

In terms of pupil remorse, I would like to witness a letter of apology to myself from a Year 11 boy, whose inappropriate greeting every time he sees me is, 'Hey Miss, how's it hanging?' and I don't think he his referring to the precarious balance of my tree. The casualness of the greeting is breathtaking. I simply can't get through to pupils the importance of the full sentence. I could give him the results of the pencil test, to satisfy his curiosity, but really the results are just too disheartening.

If only personal observations could be expressed from teacher to pupil without the threat of litigation and the services of the union, Mr Fox's final comment in the leavers' yearbook, about two of his departing form members, could be unanimously applauded. 'They need to buy belts for their future careers, otherwise gain a lot of weight, because their trousers have been hanging on for dear life for the last couple of years!'

The situation can be even more litigious if a comment is unwittingly made from a teacher to pupils concerning a fellow colleague. There was an incident, many years ago, pre the dawning of the teaching assistant (when teachers knew how to teach without any sort of assistance) that involved the deputy headteacher before Deputy Don. Well, Deputy pre-Deputy Don marched into the classroom, no reason given; blissfully unaware his flies were undone. This indiscretion caused the class more hysteria than a donkey's femidom. Quick thinking and sage words on my part, after he'd departed, were meant to calm, not inflame the situation, but take it from me, if ever you need to gain classroom control in a similar situation, don't use the line 'a dead parrot can't fall out of its cage'!

Yours truly

Beth

The Final Straw

15.12.19

Dear Cassie,

Having my world tipped upside has not been restricted to the physical; an early morning phone call, one week ago, has put me into a metaphorical tailspin.

At 7.15 am, one hour earlier than normal, Mrs Drinkwater rang up to ask if I would teach geography for the day, adding, as if I was not already aware of the difference, 'it's not PE, drama, PSE or maths.' Sweet mercies! 'And you do like teaching geography, don't you?' as if I needed some sort of persuasion.

It is true; I do enjoy teaching geography on the grounds that the department works within a specific and limited decibel range and has a plentiful supply of paper. I'm familiar with all of the geography lessons and have come across Walter so many times that I'm expecting an e-mail, 'cash only please, the more the better' for an invite to the wedding.

Usually, upon accepting the daily mission, the phone call is terminated swiftly so that a one legged, microbiologically challenged whistle blower, out of work actor, Durex featherlite rep, or previously sacked maths teacher can be found to fill the parts that others can't reach. But on this occasion, Mrs Drinkwater was hesitant and dilatory, filling the airways with idle chit chat.

In fact, she sounded as tremulous as when the PC rang up; courtesy call only, to inform us that in her own home, the tree would go up on 6th December, not the 18th, for the Christmas period, not the Christmas week. I blame a combination of the Kyle influence and keeping the wrong sort of company. Anyway, eventually Mrs Drinkwater worked up the courage of the festive fiend, promulgating a change in the law, to get the nub of the matter and present the germane facts.

Big Mac, in his infinite wisdom, with his eye, surprisingly, on the accounts than the toolbox, has advised the incoming headteacher that the school would save money by not employing the qualified supply teacher. The in-house, non-teaching cover supervisor will replace the role of the supply teacher. However, there are no flies on Big Mac; the school would still like to employ my services as a teacher, but at the rates of pay accorded the cover supervisor.

I might enjoy teaching geography but not enough to have my pay slashed, as if I were only a mere acquaintance of Walter. Moreover, neither Big Mac, nor the new headteacher, Mr Sitwell (he certainly isn't with me) have had the courtesy or common decency, after over thirty years of loyal service to the school, at the beck and call of every phone call, to tell me of their plans in person. Manners cost nothing, and so surely couldn't upset the budget. If I were setting a crossword clue, a pair of pusillanimous rodents, four letters beginning with 'r' springs to mind. And if pusillanimous has you flummoxed, I'll throw you a lifeline with a second, easier clue: a pair of pusillanimous rodents, four letters beginning with 'r' that go hand in hand with hen coop.

Having the wind knocked out of my sails is becoming a habit but with subtraction abilities speeding up (my mother keeps doing back checks) it took less than a heartbeat to inform Mrs Drinkwater (doing the bidding of others) that I would no longer be available for searching for Walter at the drop of a hat. The role and status of the supply teacher is already seriously underrated, and I absolutely refuse to denigrate it any further.

So, out of the blue, I am hanging up my pen, on a secure hook, without having to employ the services of the armed guard. An inauspicious ending, without so much as a star jump from 'cooking on gas' man, or a box of expired 'glows in the dark'. Yet, despite such a crass and ignominious dismissal, where 'thank you,' is reserved solely for the pupil, the overriding feeling I have, now that the sex, science, and sausage rolls (I never did get the chance to relay the dangers of that portable food product with an edible casing) are out of the equation, along with the quadratic and the simultaneous, is one of overwhelming relief.

To be able to see clearly, without the chartreuse fog of the science lab, and be free of the shouting, shrieking and stomach-churning smells of thirteen hundred pupils is akin to having the weight of the loft lifted off my shoulders. Or it will be, once I've devoted my newly found time to clearing it. I have been handed a list, one with my name clearly highlighted at the top.

There's no need for any family members to find jobs on my account (power hosing the flags – not a chance) because I intend to enjoy and embrace retirement, for one who will never get to see retirement, and live my life to the full. Not to lavish with details but suffice to say there are postcard albums to be catalogued and tulip bulbs don't plant themselves. I might even have the tea on the table, at the dot of five, now that the excuse 'I need to lie down in a darkened room' has gone by the by.

To occupy my days the lodger has suggested voice training lessons, not as an excuse for a tardy tea, but to lower the stentorian tone over the kitchen table, as projecting to your nearest dining neighbour is not the same as projecting to the back of the classroom containing thirty talented speakers. He needs to address his concerns to his sister; she may only have one word but knows how to cut right on through, along with the over exuberant use of door knocker despite retaining a key!

And so, my dear friend, along with my career, I am nearly at the end, with only a few more thoughts to share. In Mr Sitwell's case, 'as you sow, so shall you reap', because things can always come back to bite. I'm hoping, on a 'learning walk' – educational jargon for entering a classroom without a warrant, looking for signs of riot, which will lead him to the food technology door. He'll get his just desserts there; after all, revenge is a dish best served cold. The 'Fruit Fusion', hopefully, providing the bitter disappointment, my fault again for giving the instruction, 'you may use any fruits of your choosing', never thinking for one moment that sharp, acidic lemons and tart, tangy grapefruits would be substitutes for luscious grapes and the sweetest of strawberries.

If I could have one meaningful lesson left to share with the pupils, above all the others, including the eating (the occasional product is edible), drinking (soft drinks only), sex (safely – Double Dutch is best), and be merry lessons (emotional wellbeing – pupils trying to find themselves as well as the school bag), it would be of the importance of family. Not all pupils are blessed, as we both have been, with stalwart parents and a loving family.

I had a wonderful upbringing with parents who cared and taught me the value of life, good manners, the answer to six times eight, along with how to read using the book Kitty and Rover. My parents' deep love for each other, decency, goodness, generosity, and support has guided me throughout my life, and so when tossed like coffee dregs out of a tower block window, I have the wherewithal to still hold my head up high.

My feisty mother's most well worn of phrases is 'never be a doormat to a man', and as a result, my lovely, warm-hearted sister (looking less green than she used to), beloved daughter and I have all been able to stand our ground. Something the lodger, in my case, prefers to attribute to the incorrect protein to carbohydrate balance. (He's cutting again after bulking up, it's some sort of unfathomable gym regime.)

My greatest champion is my husband, and I wouldn't have lasted three classroom weeks, let alone thirty years without his unstinting support. He is, without doubt, my shining light, and an absolute bargain to boot, even if his spelling is rather suspect and our musical tastes poles apart. It's excruciating, as a teacher of musical taste, the sound of silence, to find a note penned in my husband's handwriting ('try harder' springs to mind), giving instructions on how to cook a roast ham for the appointed hour, 'Don't forget to cut the rapper of the ham!' I might not know about weight bearing joists but at least I know how to spell, with an overriding fondness for the silent letter.

In time, I hope the lodger and PC will find their own soul mates to provide a balance to their own career choices, should the lodger ever get out a map to find the career path. But wherever they end up (own home preferred) and whatever they do, I trust we will be there to support them – all requests in writing, letter headed note paper or quality embossed card only – no e-mails, texts, or out of hours telephone calls – for the broom, bucket and mop, or needle and thread if there is a bloody great hole!

I cannot end before I've mentioned the other family members that play an important part in my life, namely my affable brother, a kind-hearted uncle and devoted son – for many buttery reasons (he'll already be panicking in the sibling stakes because I mentioned my sister first; however, there is no pecking order, I am secure at the top and cannot be knocked off the perch) and also my nieces, nephews, and brother-in-law and sister-in-law. I hope, unlike the lodger, none of them will sue!

The same sentiment applies to 'Eloise of Lourdes', Minibus Marlene, Coconut Tuppers, racy Mrs Braithwaite, Mrs

Drinkwater, School Nurse, school caretakers, the resource ladies, the science technicians (friends past and present) and the star of the show, the resplendent Mr Honeyman, currently trimming his glad rags with a fabulous feather boa, all fine exponents of their own craft. And last, but not least, to the school's other leading light, the indomitable and perspicacious Mrs Prendergast, a thoroughly good egg, or will be when I have perfected the timings! What I wouldn't give for such a beautiful, mellifluous speaking voice. To one and all, please forgive me!

As for the rest, if only I could have said what I really thought but 'keep your thoughts to yourself' is a hard rule to break, particularly after the habits of a lifetime.

And so, my dear friend, with the stresses and strains of school life and supply teaching behind me, it is time to finally let you go and burden you no more with all my tales of woe. (Sorry, it's the pesky English department's fetish for rhyme creeping in again.) Instead, I wish to grant you the peace that you so richly deserve and thank you, once again, for believing in me and encouraging me on when I have needed encouragement the most. It is a fortunate person indeed that has their own flag bearer, and I have been blessed to have had a good number.

And so, I shall end my letter writing, as I begun, hoping to make you smile. Following my mother's maxim, 'always save the best until last' (not if the growing boy – 'he's a lad isn't he?' – as if it is some sort of achievement, is knocking around), I wish to share my favourite parental letter of all time. A letter that left me lost for words.

Dear <u>Miss</u> James,

(There has often been confusion concerning my marital status over the years, one young man disbelievingly expressing – 'you've got a husband?') Considering my penchant for collecting, the only miracle is that I haven't got a string of them. Anyway, I think I will begin this one again:

Dear Miss James,

We bought a parakeet a fortnight last Saturday, but we cannot get him to talk whatever we try. His name is Milton and we wondered if you had any ideas on helping him find his voice because our Hedley says you are good in biology. We would be grateful for any suggestions.

Sometimes, for supply teachers and parakeets alike (villains, hen owners, tongue tied drama pupils – it's an exhaustive list) 'no comment' really is the only answer!!

With eternal love and gratitude,
Your erstwhile colleague

Beth.